# THE WITHDRAWN

FASHION RETAIL
ACADEMY

# Library

Renewals: 020 7307 2365     Email: library@fra.ac.uk

D1421726

15 Gresse Street, London W1T

KOGAN
PAGE

London and Philadelphia

00002152

This book has been endorsed by the Institute of Directors.

The endorsement is given to selected Kogan Page books which the IoD recognises as being of specific interest to its members and providing them with up-to-date, informative and practical resources for creating business success. Kogan Page books endorsed by the IoD represent the most authoritative guidance available on a wide range of subjects including management, finance, marketing, training and HR.

First published in Great Britain in 2003
Paperback edition 2006

120 Pentonville Road
London N1 9JN
United Kingdom
www.kogan-page.co.uk

525 South 4th Street, #241
Philadelphia PA 19147
USA

The views expressed in this book are those of the author and are not necessarily the same as those of the Institute of Directors.

**British Library Cataloguing in Publication Data**

A CIP record for this book is available from the British Library.

ISBN 0 7494 4562 9

Typeset by JS Typesetting Ltd, Porthcawl, Mid Glamorgan
Printed and bound in Great Britain by Creative Print and Design (Wales), Ebbw Vale

# Contents

Maintenance supervisor 61; Manufacturing manager 63;
Mechanical maintenance engineer 64; Operations director
66; Process auditor 68; Process chemist 69; Process engineer
70; Product technician 71; Production engineer 72;
Production manager 74; Production operative 76;
Production planner 77; Production supervisor 79; Project
coordinator 80; Quality checker 82; Quality controller 83;
Quality manager 84; Quality systems analyst 86; Repair
technician 87; Safety manager 88; Service technician 90;
Shift coordinator 91; Technical author 92; Technical manager
93; Technical services manager 95; Technical support
engineer 96; Water engineer 97

Underwriter 170; Underwriting and claims manager 171; Underwriting clerk 173; Underwriting manager 174

# Introduction

## HOW TO USE THIS BOOK

This book consists of two main parts.

The first part, Chapters 1 to 16, contains over 200 model job descriptions, based on actual jobs and in sufficient detail to make them suitable for use in job evaluation schemes. These are separated into different categories, such as sales and marketing, for ease of reference.

The second part, Chapters 17 to 23, contains some of the common elements found in a large number of jobs, such as budgetary management and supervision. These elements are listed under the different job categories set out in the job description chapters.

To find a job description appropriate for a job in your company or organization you should find the job title in Chapters 1 to 16 that most closely matches the job you are looking for and then select any missing element from Chapters 17 to 23 and add this into the job. If, for example, you have a secretary who also has supervisory responsibilities you would select the job description for secretary from the secretarial and clerical jobs list in Chapter 14 and then add in a suitable sentence from the examples set out under the secretarial and clerical jobs category in Chapter 23, Supervision and management.

This chapter describes the features, uses, and means of building job descriptions. The aim is to provide general information about writing job descriptions suitable for your purposes.

# WHY HAVE A JOB DESCRIPTION?

A job description is a written statement of the content of any particular job and derived from the analysis of that job. It can be distinguished from a person specification, which describes not the content of the job, but the attributes required of an employee to do that job to the required standard.

Job descriptions can serve a number of useful purposes. Their main uses are set out below.

## Legal and contractual

There is no legal requirement to give an employee a job description, although there is a requirement to describe a job briefly, or to indicate the job title, in the statement of terms and conditions of employment that forms part of the employment contract. However, having an accurate and up-to-date job description can avoid ambiguity about a jobholder's responsibilities and could be valuable information when dealing with disciplinary issues or grievances. The content of any such job description will be part of the contract between the employee and the employer.

## Human resource planning

Any organization has to decide what people and skills are required to help it meet its objectives. Detailed descriptions of the objectives and tasks to be achieved together with the knowledge, skills and experience required to meet these will help to ensure that the organization is aware of the types and numbers of jobs to be filled.

## Recruitment and selection

Before any job can be filled it is essential to have a clear idea of the requirements of that job. Without this information it is difficult to decide what qualifications, experience and personal attributes might be required and to determine the appropriate salary level. A job description and a person specification will provide the required information and assist managers in deciding on the most appropriate selection process.

## Job evaluation

Any job evaluation exercise is critically dependent on having accurate information about jobs. Inevitably, this means producing job descriptions.

## Training and development

It is important to identify the content of jobs when analysing training needs, as without this information it will be difficult to specify the outputs, standards of performance and competencies required. When accurate job information is available, any mismatch between the expected outputs from the job and individual performance is easier to identify.

## Job redesign

Change is a permanent feature of all organizations and with an increased emphasis on allowing employees to work flexibly – it is now a legal right for an employee to be able to request flexible working arrangements – employers have to give serious consideration to different ways of working. To make such decisions effectively, sound information is required about the activities currently undertaken within jobs.

## Performance management

Performance management is a process for ensuring that the performance of individual jobholders is effectively managed and that they carry out their roles to the best of their ability and to the standards required by the organization. To measure and appraise performance effectively it is necessary to compare the requirements of the job with the extent to which the employee meets those requirements. This requires that job objectives are clearly specified, as without such clarity any performance management process will not be fully effective.

## Organization change

When organization structures and reporting lines are being changed, it is important to have good information about the content of all jobs. In this way, duplications and overlaps of responsibility can be identified and managers can ensure that no vital processes or tasks are overlooked.

## Limitations of job descriptions

1. Job descriptions describe the requirements of the job but take no account of how the individual carries out that job. It is a fact of life that different people will do the same job in different ways. In some cases this might mean that tasks and accountabilities are added to the core job description and in other cases some of these may be neglected. The emphasis placed on different aspects of the job will depend on the background and experience of the jobholder.

2. In modern organizations, especially those using project teams, individuals may be used very flexibly and more in accordance with their abilities than in terms of the specific job they were originally employed to do. This can be difficult to reflect in a job description.

3. If job descriptions are applied too rigidly they may become inappropriate for an organization that is rapidly changing.

4. Job descriptions require frequent updating because over time the work actually carried out by the jobholder may become significantly different from the responsibilities set out in the job description.

5. The quality of a job description will often depend on the writing skills and personal perceptions of the person preparing it. This is likely to be a critical issue where the job description is used for job evaluation.

The best way of combating these problems is to try to ensure that job descriptions are written flexibly by focusing on the overall objectives, rather than on the tasks to be carried out to meet those objectives, and to update them regularly. Where individuals change the job content, the job description should be amended to take these changes into account if they are intended to become a permanent feature of the job.

## JOB DESCRIPTION FEATURES

The job descriptions contained in this book are all based on actual jobs but have been rewritten as far as necessary to ensure that they are based on accountabilities, rather than just tasks. This is an important distinction because it means that the focus is on the outputs produced by the jobs rather than on the actions carried out to achieve those outputs. To illustrate this, rather than stating that a key function is 'to respond to telephone inquiries' we might instead describe that function as 'to provide information and advice by telephone to assist system users in resolving problems'.

The format of these accountability statements is to describe what is done, what it is done to, and for what purpose. Describing jobs in this way makes the job descriptions particularly suitable for job evaluation and performance management purposes.

There are of course some jobs that exist only to carry out straightforward tasks and in these cases it will be the actions carried out that form the core content of the job description.

The knowledge, skills and experience requirements, which may more accurately be described as elements of the person specification, are also based on actual jobs, but have been edited to provide general information which can be adapted to the needs of a variety of organizations.

## Excluded jobs

The job descriptions in this book are for jobs commonly found in a range of organizations, although there are also a limited number of less common jobs. Jobs that have been specifically excluded are the highly specialized roles found in public sector organizations such as local authorities, NHS Trusts and the police service. These have been excluded because in many cases the work carried out is already described in depth by statutes and by relevant professional bodies, and also because such organizations normally have the resources to prepare their own job descriptions.

# WRITING A JOB DESCRIPTION

There are no hard and fast rules about precisely what the content of a job description should be, but the headings below describe what is commonly included.

## Job identification

This includes the title of the job, the department or section, any employee or job number and the name of the jobholder (commonly omitted in a job evaluation exercise to preserve objectivity). The precise title of the job should be described briefly but accurately.

## Reporting line

This will include the title of the job to which this one directly reports.

## Organization structure

Job descriptions can contain an extract from an organization chart showing the job's reporting relationships, including subordinate posts. Alternatively, a copy of the relevant organization chart may be attached to the job description. This information is particularly relevant when the job description is required as part of a job evaluation review. The numbers and levels of jobs reporting to the jobholder are important information for job evaluation.

## Main purpose of the job

The job description should set out, in no more than one or two sentences, the key purpose of the job and this should clearly distinguish it from any other jobs in the organization.

## Principal accountabilities or responsibilities

This is very much the core of the job description and should set out the activities and actions required of the jobholder. Generally, there should be no more than about 10 such statements, although there will be more for certain jobs, as a number significantly in excess of this either means that the job description is going into too much detail or that the job is overloaded.

To prepare these you should:

- identify the key areas of responsibility within the job;
- identify what end-results have to be produced to achieve the main purpose of the job. These are the results or objectives on which the jobholder would expect to have his or her performance judged. As far as possible these should be written in terms that are suggestive of measurement;
- describe how these end-results are achieved.

The statements should be written in the following form:

| **What is done** | **to what** | **with what end result?** |
|---|---|---|
| To check | invoices | to ensure that they correspond with orders received |
| To direct and control | the staff of the section | to ensure that they are well motivated and trained |
| To prepare | minutes of all committee meetings | to ensure that they provide an accurate record of discussions and resulting decisions |

## Performance measures and standards

Performance criteria will need to be included where job descriptions are being used to define targets as part of a performance management process. The information to be included is the output expected from the job and the standards to which it is to be performed. These are commonly described as key result areas.

## Constraints

Job descriptions will sometimes set out the limits of authority and decision making for a particular job.

## Statistics

Particularly where job descriptions are used for job evaluation or performance management purposes, there may be a need to include relevant numerical and financial data. Under the Hay Guide Chart and Profile Method of Job Evaluation, for example, the financial magnitude of accountabilities is a key factor in the evaluation process, generally described as the 'dimensions' of the job. This information will include details of any budgets, equipment or other resources the jobholder is responsible for, or any data relating to outputs and workload.

## Nature and scope

Job descriptions often contain a section that describes the context of the job in the organization. This will contain, for example, information about how the job relates to others in the organization, where work comes from and where it goes to, the kinds of problems dealt with and decisions made etc.

## Contacts

Many job evaluation schemes take into account the nature and range of contacts a particular job might have. Where a job description is prepared for job evaluation purposes, therefore, it may be necessary to include a section with this information. It should include the main lines of communication of the job with other jobs in the organization and with external individuals and organizations, with the reasons for those links listed. Using the word 'liaison' in this context is particularly unhelpful as it can mean anything from high-powered negotiation to sending people copies of documents.

## Working conditions

Job evaluation schemes often also take into account the physical content of any job and the nature of the working environment and this information needs to be included to assist the evaluation process.

## Knowledge, skills and experience

While the knowledge, qualifications, skills and experience required to do the job are strictly part of a person specification, rather than a job description, it is useful to include them in one composite document which can then be used for a variety of purposes. This should describe what is required for full and effective performance of the job, not what the jobholder actually has.

## Competencies

Competencies are the personal characteristics and qualities of individuals that enable them to perform their jobs effectively. They can take the form of deep-seated traits or observable skills and behaviours. The key is to try to describe them in such away that they can be measured.

## Other information

There is often scope in job descriptions to include miscellaneous additional information, such as training requirements or responsibilities that may not be a permanent feature of the job. In some cases jobholders may have additional roles which are personal to them but which would not necessarily be expected of a new incumbent. Any such situation needs to be made clear in the job description.

## Signatures and date

Any job description should be signed by both the jobholder and his or her direct line manager to indicate that it is an agreed document and, in view of how quickly such documents can become out of date, the date of its completion is highly relevant.

# Part 1

# Job descriptions

# Administration and management

This section includes job descriptions for the following jobs:

1. Awards/grants officer
2. Business development director
3. Central services supervisor
4. Chauffeur
5. Chief executive
6. Committee administrator
7. Company secretary
8. Courier
9. Director of central services
10. Management consultant
11. Managing director
12. Member services manager
13. Nursery assistant
14. Nursery manager
15. Office maintenance worker
16. Office manager
17. VDU operator

# 1. AWARDS/GRANTS OFFICER

## Main purpose of job

To review applications for awards or grants and communicate decisions to applicants.

## Main responsibilities

1. Review applications received for grants or awards to ensure that they meet the organization's criteria and recommend action as appropriate.
2. Contact applicants as necessary to clarify points in applications and record the results of these contacts.
3. Provide advice to applicants and potential applicants about award and grant requirements and how to complete applications.
4. Respond to any general enquiries from applicants about applying for grants and awards.
5. Maintain all necessary records of applications made and the results of these.
6. Notify applicants of the outcome of their applications.
7. Set up and maintain any necessary processes to ensure that applications are monitored and controlled and dealt with in accordance with recommended criteria and timescales.
8. Maintain up-to-date knowledge of the rules relating to the allocation of grants and awards.

## Knowledge, skills and experience required

The job requires:

- education to A-level standard;
- detailed knowledge of grant scheme rules;
- at least 1 year's experience of operating a grant scheme;
- good interpersonal skills;
- organizational skills.

# 2. BUSINESS DEVELOPMENT DIRECTOR

## Main purpose of job

To develop and implement strategies, policies and processes to improve operations and service delivery to meet existing and future corporate objectives.

## Main responsibilities

1. Lead in the development of strategies, policies and processes across all functions that will help to achieve the company's mission and core objectives.

2. Recruit and motivate business-orientated teams accountable for the achievement of corporate and individual targets, ensuring that comprehensive performance appraisal and development opportunities are provided in accordance with the company's human resources strategy and employment policies.

3. Provide advice and guidance to managers and staff on all aspects of business transformation.

4. Maintain regular contact with customers to keep them aware of business developments and to seek feedback from them so that the company can effectively implement a programme of continuous improvement.

5. Develop and implement policies to recruit and retain the required levels and quality of staff to ensure that planned changes are effectively implemented and corporate objectives met.

6. Develop and control multidisciplinary teams to ensure that action plans are implemented and changes achieved that will support the organization's core objectives.

7. Develop and monitor budgets for all major organization development projects.

8. Negotiate contracts with external consultants and other organizations to provide services in support of organization change and development where these cannot be met from in-house resources.

9. Develop close working relationships with other key functions in the organization to keep them aware of, and seek their views on, proposed organizational changes to ensure that there is a coordinated approach to these.

10. Develop and implement all necessary information technology policies and processes to ensure that these support the business transformation process.
11. Maintain an awareness of any possible threats to the business and develop policies and processes that will provide for such contingencies.
12. Maintain an awareness of developments in the fields of organization change and development to ensure that the company continues to take advantage of the latest thinking in these areas.
13. Commission research in the field of organization development and change to ensure that the company implements policies and approaches that will improve operational effectiveness.

## Knowledge, skills and experience required

The job requires:

- education to degree level;
- professional qualifications in a relevant discipline;
- considerable experience of managing organization change;
- at least 5 years' senior management experience;
- knowledge of IT systems;
- excellent interpersonal skills;
- excellent analytical skills;
- excellent written and verbal communication skills.

# 3. CENTRAL SERVICES SUPERVISOR

## Main purpose of job

To supervise the provision of clerical, typing, reception and secretarial support services for a group of staff in an office or unit.

## Main responsibilities

1. Supervise all clerical, typing, secretarial and support staff to ensure that they are appropriately trained and carry out their responsibilities to the required standards.
2. Oversee the opening and distribution of internal and external post.
3. Supervise reception and switchboard staff to ensure that there is appropriate cover at all times.
4. Supervise the provision of work processing and typing services to all staff.
5. Monitor stationery and post requirements to ensure that there are adequate supplies provided at all times.
6. Consult client staff and functions to ensure that the services they require are being provided to the right standards.
7. Oversee the provision of a comprehensive and reliable filing and photocopying service.
8. Carry out secretarial and clerical duties as required to ensure that the service requirements of client staff are met.

## Knowledge, skills and experience required

The job requires:

- education to GCSE level;
- at least 2 years' experience as a word processor operator or secretary;
- supervisory experience;
- wide experience of office work;
- organizational skills;
- good interpersonal skills.

## 4. CHAUFFEUR

## Main purpose of job

To drive company executives, ensuring that they arrive at their destinations punctually and safely, and to maintain the company car(s).

## Main responsibilities

1.  Drive company executives, ensuring that they arrive at their destinations punctually and safely.
2.  Carry out all necessary safety checks and routine servicing of car, eg checking oil and water levels, tyre pressures etc.
3.  Maintain car in a clean condition, inside and out.
4.  Carry out minor repairs where necessary.
5.  Maintain mileage and car service records.

## Knowledge, skills and experience required

The job requires:

- a full clean and current UK driving licence;
- previous experience as a chauffeur;
- good interpersonal skills;
- tact and discretion.

# 5. CHIEF EXECUTIVE

## Main purpose of job

To direct and control the organization and to give strategic guidance and direction to the management and staff to ensure that the organization achieves its mission and objectives.

## Main responsibilities

1.  Direct and control the work and resources of the organization and ensure the recruitment and retention of the required numbers and types of well-motivated, trained and developed staff to ensure that it achieves its mission and objectives.
2.  Prepare a corporate plan and annual business plan and monitor progress against these plans to ensure that the organization attains its objectives as cost-effectively and efficiently as possible.
3.  Provide strategic advice and guidance to the Board and senior managers, to keep them aware of developments within the industry and to ensure that the appropriate policies are developed to meet the organization's mission and objectives and to comply with all relevant statutory and other regulations.
4.  Establish and maintain effective formal and informal links with major customers, relevant government departments and agencies, local authorities, key decision-makers and other stakeholders generally, to exchange information and views and to ensure that the organization is providing the appropriate range and quality of services.
5.  Develop and maintain research and development programmes to ensure that the organization remains at the forefront of its sector, applies the most cost-effective methods and approaches, and provides the required range and quality of services.
6.  Prepare, gain acceptance, and monitor the implementation of the annual budget to ensure that budget targets are met, that revenue flows are maximized and that fixed costs are minimized.
7.  Develop and maintain an effective marketing and public relations strategy to promote the products, services and image of the organization in the wider community.

8.  Represent the organization in negotiations with customers, suppliers, government departments and other key contacts to secure the most effective contract terms for the organization.
9.  Develop and maintain total quality management systems throughout the organization to ensure that the best possible products and services are provided to customers and/or clients.
10. Develop, promote and direct the implementation of equal opportunities policies in all aspects of the organization.
11. Oversee the preparation of the annual report and accounts of the organization and ensure their approval.
12. Develop and direct the implementation of policies and procedures to ensure that the organization complies with all health and safety and other statutory regulations.

## Knowledge, skills and experience required

The job requires:

- a proven record of success in senior-level general or commercial management, preferably in a related industry;
- at least 10 years' senior-level experience of management of people and resources;
- graduate level of intellect, preferably with a higher degree in a management discipline or a professional qualification;
- a wide knowledge of the sector;
- an understanding of financial management and wider management principles and techniques;
- political and presentational skills with an appreciation of the demands of conflicting interests and of meeting statutory requirements;
- a very high level of financial and commercial awareness;
- leadership skills;
- excellent communication skills;
- excellent organizational skills;
- excellent analytical and problem-solving skills.

# 6. COMMITTEE ADMINISTRATOR

## Main purpose of job

To coordinate all arrangements for the effective administration of committee procedures.

## Main responsibilities

1. Prepare agendas for committee meetings and ensure that these are printed and despatched to committee members at the agreed times.
2. Attend meetings of committees and prepare notes and minutes arising from those meetings to agreed standards and timetables.
3. Take follow-up action after committee meetings to ensure that decisions made are implemented and so that results can be reported back to future meetings.
4. Maintain contact with all relevant managers and staff to ensure that matters to be reported to committees are included on the appropriate agendas.
5. Prepare reports on various matters for the information of the committee.
6. Advise the chair and committee members on correct committee procedure.
7. Maintain an awareness of matters relevant to the committee and ensure that reports and information of interest are brought to the attention of committee members.
8. Prepare reports and statements on behalf of the committee to represent their views to the media.

## Knowledge, skills and experience required

The job requires:

- a degree-level qualification;
- ideally a professional qualification equivalent to ICSA;
- at least 2 years' experience of committee administration;
- sound knowledge of committee procedures;
- ability to write clearly and concisely;
- good interpersonal skills.

# 7. COMPANY SECRETARY

## Main purpose of job

To coordinate all arrangements for meetings of the Board to ensure that they are properly organized and conducted, and to implement all necessary policies and procedures to ensure that the company complies with the Memorandum, Articles of Association and its statutory obligations.

## Main responsibilities

1.  Coordinate all arrangements for meetings of the Board and management committees to ensure that they are properly organized and conducted and that minutes are accurately recorded and circulated.
2.  Advise the Board and management committees on all statutory and constitutional requirements to ensure that business is conducted in a proper and effective manner.
3.  Circulate decisions of the Board and committees to all relevant parties and take any necessary follow-up action to record progress on these.
4.  Keep Board and committee members informed of all issues relevant to them and provide any necessary training and induction to ensure that they are aware of their responsibilities and of procedure.
5.  Prepare any returns and records required by statute to ensure that the organization conducts its business in a legal and proper manner.
6.  Prepare the annual report of the organization in accordance with legal and constitutional requirements.
7.  Maintain the share register and the membership records of the Board and management committees.
8.  Oversee the arrangements for the conduct of elections to the Board and committees.
9.  Take all necessary steps to ensure that the company complies with data protection legislation.
10. Provide all necessary advice on mergers and acquisitions, ensuring that a thorough risk analysis is carried out.

# Knowledge, skills and experience required

The job requires:

- a qualified company secretary or lawyer;
- at least 10 years' experience as a company secretary or lawyer;
- good knowledge of the organization;
- excellent organizational and time management skills;
- good interpersonal skills.

# 8. COURIER

## Main purpose of job

To operate an internal courier service by collecting and delivering post and other items.

## Main responsibilities

1. Collect all internal mail from offices and other internal sites in accordance with a prescribed schedule.
2. Deliver mail to all internal sites in accordance with a prescribed schedule.
3. Carry out ad hoc deliveries of items as required from time to time.
4. Assist in sorting post and in receiving goods and parcels.

## Knowledge, skills and experience required

The job requires:

- a sound basic education;
- honesty and reliability;
- an ability to work without supervision.

## 9. DIRECTOR OF CENTRAL SERVICES

## Main purpose of job

To direct and control all central administrative services to ensure that the company continues to function effectively and efficiently.

## Main responsibilities

1. Direct and control the staff of the department to ensure that they are appropriately motivated and trained and that they carry out their responsibilities to the required standards.
2. Develop and implement all necessary administrative policies and procedures to ensure that the company continues to operate efficiently and effectively.
3. Direct and control all central services to ensure that they provide managers and staff with the level of support they require.
4. Monitor the performance of all central services to ensure that they operate to a high standard and to identify any areas of potential improvement.
5. Provide committee services to the company, including the preparation and distribution of agendas, reports and minutes.
6. Develop and control the annual budget for all central support services.
7. Provide a full company secretarial service to the company, ensuring that all statutory requirements are met.
8. Develop and implement any necessary information technology systems to ensure that administrative processes operate as efficiently and effectively as possible.
9. Develop all necessary procedures to ensure that all the company's offices and equipment are maintained to a high standard and provide a safe and healthy working environment.
10. Develop and implement all necessary policies and procedures to ensure that correct procedures are followed by managers and staff in appointing consultants, contractors or other suppliers.
11. Negotiate contracts as necessary for the effective maintenance of buildings and equipment.

12. Develop and implement a central record-keeping and information service and ensure that all necessary safeguards are in place to maintain data security.
13. Advise managers and staff of the administrative support implications of operational changes.
14. Maintain an awareness of any legislative or other changes that might affect the provision of central support services to ensure that the company continues to comply with all relevant statutory and regulatory requirements.

## Knowledge, skills and experience required

The job requires:

- education to degree level;
- a suitable professional qualification;
- at least 10 years' experience of providing central support services;
- considerable management experience;
- a good knowledge of all relevant legislation, particularly in relation to office premises and health and safety;
- knowledge of company law;
- knowledge of finance and budgets;
- excellent interpersonal skills;
- excellent organization skills.

# 10. MANAGEMENT CONSULTANT

## Main purpose of job

To analyse problems, and provide advice and guidance to a range of organizations on issues and problems relating to policies, organization, procedures and methods and to recommend appropriate actions, providing assistance with implementation where required.

## Main responsibilities

1. Carry out market research to identify consultancy opportunities.
2. Prepare presentations and proposals to prospective clients to sell consultancy projects.
3. Analyse client requirements and determine the most appropriate consultancy approach to meet these.
4. Identify and carry out all necessary research to define client problems.
5. Carry out research, analyse problems and identify potential solutions for a variety of client projects to present workable solutions or provide specialist advice to enable clients to resolve business problems.
6. Prepare and present reports setting out the findings, conclusions and recommendations arising from consultancy projects.
7. Maintain regular contact with the client to ensure that there is regular information about project progress.
8. Assist with implementation of consultancy recommendations as required, including providing any necessary training to client staff.
9. Maintain all required project and client data to ensure that full information is available for project planning, contract management and business development.
10. Maintain an awareness of developments in relevant field of expertise to ensure that advice given is accurate and up to date.
11. Develop and implement all required administrative and financial systems and data to ensure that accurate financial and statutory records can be maintained.

## Knowledge, skills and experience required

The job requires:

- education to degree level;
- ideally, a higher qualification or a suitable professional qualification;
- at least 5 years' general management experience;
- specialist expertise in a specific management discipline;
- a broad understanding of management theory and techniques;
- excellent analytical skills;
- excellent interpersonal skills;
- excellent written and verbal communication skills;
- excellent negotiating and sales skills;
- excellent organizational skills;
- decision-making skills;
- time management skills.

# 11. MANAGING DIRECTOR

## Main purpose of job

To direct and control the company's operations and to give strategic guidance and direction to the Board to ensure that the company achieves its mission and objectives.

## Main responsibilities

1. Direct and control the work and resources of the company and ensure the recruitment and retention of the required numbers and types of well-motivated, trained and developed staff to ensure that it achieves its mission and objectives.

2. Prepare a corporate plan and annual business plan and monitor progress against these plans to ensure that the company attains its objectives as cost-effectively and efficiently as possible.

3. Provide strategic advice and guidance to the chairman and the members of the Board, to keep them aware of developments within the industry and to ensure that the appropriate policies are developed to meet the company's mission and objectives and to comply with all relevant statutory and other regulations.

4. Establish and maintain effective formal and informal links with major customers, relevant government departments and agencies, local authorities, key decision-makers and other stakeholders generally, to exchange information and views and to ensure that the company is providing the appropriate range and quality of services.

5. Develop and maintain research and development programmes to ensure that the company remains at the forefront in the industry, applies the most cost-effective methods and approaches, provides leading-edge products and services, and retains its competitive edge.

6. Prepare, gain acceptance, and monitor the implementation of the annual budget to ensure that budget targets are met, that revenue flows are maximized and that fixed costs are minimized.

7. Develop and maintain an effective marketing and public relations strategy to promote the products, services and image of the company in the wider community.

8. Represent the company in negotiations with customers, suppliers, government departments and other key contacts to secure the most effective contract terms for the company.

9. Develop and maintain total quality management systems throughout the company to ensure that the best possible products and services are provided to customers.

10. Develop, promote and direct the implementation of equal opportunities policies in all aspects of the company's work.

11. Prepare the annual report and accounts of the company and ensure their approval by the Board.

12. Develop and direct the implementation of policies and procedures to ensure that the company complies with all health and safety and other statutory regulations.

## Knowledge, skills and experience required

The job requires:

- a proven record of success in senior-level general or commercial management, preferably in a related industry;
- at least 10 years' senior-level experience of management of people and resources;
- graduate level of intellect, preferably with a higher degree in a management discipline or a professional qualification;
- a wide knowledge of the industry;
- an understanding of financial management and wider management principles and techniques;
- political and presentational skills with an appreciation of the demands of conflicting interests and of meeting statutory requirements;
- a very high level of commercial awareness;
- leadership skills;
- excellent communication skills;
- excellent organizational skills;
- excellent analytical and problem-solving skills.

## 12. MEMBER SERVICES MANAGER

## Main purpose of job

To recruit and provide services and support to members of an association.

## Main responsibilities

1. Recruit new members to the association to ensure the continued and increasing influence of the association.
2. Provide support and advice to new and existing members to ensure that they gain the maximum benefit from membership of the association.
3. Contribute to the development of association policies which reflect the needs and objectives of association members.
4. Maintain regular contact with members to obtain feedback about their needs and objectives and their opinions of the services provided by the association.
5. Maintain an accurate and up-to-date database of existing and potential members and ensure that this data is maintained in accordance with data protection principles.
6. Arrange and attend meetings of groups of members at local and national levels to discuss topics of interest to them and the association and arrange social functions.
7. Act as a conciliator between members in the event of disputes.
8. Produce regular publications to keep members informed of association activities and other matters of interest to them.
9. Represent the association at external events to promote the image of the association and to increase membership.
10. Maintain regular contact with external agencies to promote the use of the association and its members.

## Knowledge, skills and experience required

The job requires:

- education to degree level;
- experience within the industry;

- detailed knowledge of the association and its services;
- at least 3 years' experience in a membership services role;
- excellent interpersonal and promotional skills;
- presentation skills;
- organizational skills;
- negotiating skills.

# 13. NURSERY ASSISTANT

## Main purpose of job

To assist in running a daytime nursery which provides a safe, caring and stimulating environment for children.

## Main responsibilities

1.  Assist in the day-to-day running of the nursery to provide a safe caring and stimulating environment for children.
2.  Provide suitable toys and games to encourage learning and play.
3.  Provide food and drink to children as necessary.
4.  Provide assistance to children as necessary to ensure that they are well cared for.
5.  Assist in cleaning the nursery to ensure that cleanliness and hygiene are maintained to the required standards.

## Knowledge, skills and experience required

The job requires:

- a basic childcare qualification;
- experience of working in a nursery;
- knowledge of nursery practice and procedures;
- good interpersonal skills.

# 14. NURSERY MANAGER

## Main purpose of job

To organize a daytime nursery which provides a safe, caring and stimulating environment for children.

## Main responsibilities

1. Organize the nursery on a day-to-day basis, ensuring that it provides a safe, caring and stimulating environment for children and complies with all relevant Regulations.
2. Allocate nursery places as required with the aim of achieving the maximum usage consistent with maintaining high standards of care and supervision.
3. Plan and implement a wide variety of learning programmes and experiences to stimulate the interests and encourage the development of children.
4. Supervise and train the staff of the nursery to ensure that they carry out their responsibilities to the required standards.
5. Recommend to management any changes that might be required to develop or improve the services provided.
6. Maintain stocks of consumables, and accept payments, keeping any necessary records.
7. Maintain all required records of children and their attendance.
8. Promote good working relationships with both internal and external bodies to ensure that an awareness is maintained of the latest childcare practices and Regulations and to promote the image of the nursery as a care provider for children.
9. Notify parents of any issues that may need to be drawn to their attention.

## Knowledge, skills and experience required

The job requires:

- a certificate in childcare;
- at least 5 years' experience in childcare;
- experience of working in a day nursery;

- practical understanding of the physical and emotional needs of children and parents;
- supervisory experience;
- detailed knowledge of nursery practice and procedures;
- excellent interpersonal skills;
- a first aid qualification;
- a food hygiene certificate.

# 15. OFFICE MAINTENANCE WORKER

(See also 'maintenance worker' in the estates and surveying job descriptions)

## Main purpose of job

To carry out maintenance and repair tasks, supervise cleaning arrangements and take all steps necessary to ensure the security of the company's offices.

## Main responsibilities

1. Carry out minor repairs to office buildings and furniture.
2. Inspect office buildings and premises and report any areas requiring maintenance or repair.
3. Get quotations from suppliers and external contractors for goods and services relating to the maintenance of the offices and which cannot be supplied internally.
4. Maintain a record of reports and complaints from staff relating to the building and its fixtures and fittings.
5. Take all necessary actions as a registered key-holder to ensure the safety and security of the building.
6. Supervise the office cleaning work carried out by in-house staff or by contractors to ensure that it is carried out to the required standards.
7. Arrange regular fire drills and ensure that all fire-fighting equipment is correctly maintained.
8. Carry out minor decorating work.
9. Assist with moving furniture, and porterage as required.
10. Maintain the car park and office grounds in a reasonable condition.

## Knowledge, skills and experience required

The job requires:

- a basic level of education;
- practical skills;
- good knowledge of the office building.

# 16. OFFICE MANAGER

## Main purpose of job

To ensure that the company's office building is maintained as a cost-effective, safe and secure environment and to ensure the effective provision of office services to company staff.

## Main responsibilities

1.  Draw up schedules for the periodic inspection and maintenance of offices and monitor any work undertaken to ensure that it is to the required standards.
2.  Negotiate and agree services with contractors to ensure that repairs and regular maintenance are carried out.
3.  Monitor the performance of contractors to ensure that work is carried out to the required standards.
4.  Introduce all necessary procedures to ensure the security of the building.
5.  Negotiate and agree cleaning services for the building and monitor the work carried out to ensure that it is of the required standard.
6.  Supervise the work of administrative support staff to ensure that they provide the administrative services required by the company to the required standards.
7.  Negotiate contracts for the purchase of stationery and office equipment on the most cost-effective basis.
8.  Supervise the distribution of incoming mail and the efficient despatch of outgoing mail.
9.  Carry out routine inspections to ensure that first aid boxes are adequately stocked and that fire extinguishers are correctly maintained.
10. Keep all staff informed of office procedures.
11. Maintain all necessary records to ensure that the office is well maintained, that administrative services are provided as required and that invoices are processed for work carried out.
12. Prepare the annual budget for office services and monitor expenditure against this budget.

13.  Maintain an awareness of the best practice in office procedures and of developments in office technology to ensure the continued effective and efficient running of the company's offices.

## Knowledge, skills and experience required

The job requires:

- qualifications to GCSE A-level standard;
- at least 2 years' office management experience;
- a good knowledge of all office systems;
- supervisory experience;
- excellent interpersonal skills;
- excellent organization skills.

# 17. VDU OPERATOR

## Main purpose of job

To input and extract data quickly and accurately using a VDU or computer terminal.

## Main responsibilities

1. Enter standard documents into the computer quickly and accurately using the keyboard.
2. Check data entered for accuracy and refer any queries to supervisor or data originator.
3. Select appropriate program or software for data being entered.
4. Report any data entry problems to supervisor.

## Knowledge, skills and experience required

The job requires:

- education to GCSE level;
- keyboard skills;
- general knowledge of the functions carried out.

# 2

# Engineering and production

This section includes job descriptions for the following jobs:

1. Chief electrical engineer
2. Chief mechanical engineer
3. Civil engineer
4. Contract manager
5. Design manager
6. Development engineer
7. Draughtsperson
8. Electrical engineer
9. Electrical technician
10. Environmental manager
11. Factory manager
12. Hygiene officer
13. Maintenance supervisor
14. Manufacturing manager
15. Mechanical maintenance engineer
16. Operations director

17. Process auditor
18. Process chemist
19. Process engineer
20. Product technician
21. Production engineer
22. Production manager
23. Production operative
24. Production planner
25. Production supervisor
26. Project coordinator
27. Quality checker
28. Quality controller
29. Quality manager
30. Quality systems analyst
31. Repair technician
32. Safety manager
33. Service technician
34. Shift coordinator
35. Technical author
36. Technical manager
37. Technical services manager
38. Technical support engineer
39. Water engineer

# 1. CHIEF ELECTRICAL ENGINEER

## Main purpose of job

Direct and control the company's electrical engineering function to ensure the provision of a comprehensive maintenance and engineering service so that all processes, plant, equipment and buildings are developed and maintained to agreed standards.

## Main responsibilities

1.  Direct and control the staff of the electrical engineering function to ensure that all processes, plant, equipment and buildings are maintained to agreed standards.
2.  Develop the department's budget in discussion with other managers and maintain any necessary systems and processes to ensure effective budget monitoring and control.
3.  Monitor electrical maintenance work to ensure that it is carried out to the required standard and within agreed budget levels.
4.  Direct and control electrical engineering projects to ensure that they are completed to the standards required within agreed timescales and to the agreed budget level.
5.  Provide expert technical advice on all aspects of electrical engineering to other managers and staff to ensure effective decision making.
6.  Develop the company's strategy in relation to engineering and ensure that all maintenance standards are adhered to by staff and contractors.
7.  Maintain knowledge of modern maintenance techniques, machinery, processes and equipment and recommend any new systems that will enhance the effectiveness of the engineering function.
8.  Recruit, train and motivate maintenance staff to ensure that they carry out their responsibilities to the required standards.
9.  Ensure that all electrical maintenance engineering activities are carried out in accordance with the company's health and safety requirements and in compliance with relevant health and safety legislation.

10. Investigate and resolve any disciplinary or employee relations issues to ensure that all processes, plant and equipment continue to be maintained to the standards necessary to meet operational requirements.

## Knowledge, skills and experience required

The job requires:

- a degree in electrical engineering;
- qualification as a chartered engineer;
- a minimum of 10 years' electrical engineering experience;
- knowledge of the industry;
- experience of managing teams in a technical environment;
- an ability to solve technical problems;
- good human relations, motivational and communication skills;
- knowledge of modern maintenance techniques;
- project management skills.

## 2. CHIEF MECHANICAL ENGINEER

### Main purpose of job

Direct and control the company's mechanical engineering function to ensure the provision of a comprehensive maintenance and engineering service so that all processes, plant, equipment and buildings are developed and maintained to agreed standards.

### Main responsibilities

1. Direct and control the staff of the mechanical engineering function to ensure that all processes, plant, equipment and buildings are maintained to agreed standards.
2. Develop the department's budget in discussion with other managers and maintain any necessary systems and processes to ensure effective budget monitoring and control.
3. Monitor mechanical maintenance work to ensure that it is carried out to the required standard and within agreed budget levels.
4. Direct and control mechanical engineering projects to ensure that they are completed to the standards required within agreed timescales and to the agreed budget level.
5. Provide expert technical advice on all aspects of mechanical engineering to other managers and staff to ensure effective decision making.
6. Develop the company's strategy in relation to engineering and ensure that all maintenance standards are adhered to by staff and contractors.
7. Maintain knowledge of modern maintenance techniques, machinery, processes and equipment and recommend any new systems that will enhance the effectiveness of the engineering function.
8. Recruit, train and motivate maintenance staff to ensure that they carry out their responsibilities to the required standards.
9. Ensure that all mechanical maintenance engineering activities are carried out in accordance with the company's health and safety requirements and in compliance with relevant health and safety legislation.

10. Investigate and resolve any disciplinary or employee relations issues to ensure that all processes, plant and equipment continue to be maintained to the standards necessary to meet operational requirements.

## Knowledge, skills and experience required

The job requires:

- a degree in mechanical engineering;
- qualification as a chartered engineer;
- a minimum of 10 years' electrical engineering experience;
- a knowledge of the industry;
- experience of managing teams in a technical environment;
- an ability to solve technical problems;
- good human relations, motivational and communication skills;
- knowledge of modern maintenance techniques;
- project management skills.

# 3. CIVIL ENGINEER

## Main purpose of job

To provide advice and expertise to managers and staff on all civil engineering aspects of the company's operations.

## Main responsibilities

1. Provide technical advice to managers and staff on all aspects of civil engineering relating to the company's operations.
2. Carry out any required site visits and inspections to determine the civil engineering aspects of planned works.
3. Carry out feasibility studies for major and minor works and recommend new projects and extensions to existing projects.
4. Direct and control civil engineering projects to ensure that they are completed to the standards required within agreed timescales and to the agreed budget level.
5. Advise on the purchase of plant and machinery to ensure that it is appropriate for the purposes intended.
6. Maintain regular contact with other professionals and staff involved in large engineering projects to ensure that there is effective overall coordination.
7. Prepare reports on the civil engineering aspects of projects to ensure that decisions are based on the best possible information and take account of all resource implications and time and budgetary constraints.
8. Maintain knowledge of modern civil engineering techniques and processes and recommend any new systems that will enhance the effectiveness of the civil engineering function.

## Knowledge, skills and experience required

The job requires:

- a degree in civil engineering;
- qualification as a civil engineer;
- a minimum of 5 years' civil engineering experience;
- a knowledge of the industry;

- experience of supervising teams in a technical environment;
- an ability to solve technical problems;
- good human relations, motivational and communication skills;
- project management skills.

# 4. CONTRACT MANAGER

## Main purpose of job

To coordinate the installation of company products and systems to ensure that the company meets its contractual obligations to the customers' complete satisfaction.

## Main responsibilities

1. Plan the installation of products and services to ensure that these are completed to the required standards and within the agreed timescale.
2. Inspect completed installations to ensure that these have been undertaken to the required standards.
3. Maintain regular contact with installers and subcontractors to ensure that they are appropriately trained and carry out contract work to the required standards.
4. Respond to any customer complaints to ensure that these are dealt with speedily and effectively.
5. Monitor all installation costs to ensure that these are within agreed budget limits.
6. Discuss product enhancements and potential variations to the contract with customers to maximize sales revenue.
7. Maintain all necessary records to ensure the effective monitoring of contracts.

## Knowledge, skills and experience required

The job requires:

- qualifications equivalent to ONC, NVQ level III;
- at least 2 years' experience of managing contracts;
- thorough knowledge of the company's products and processes;
- good communication skills;
- good analytical skills;
- good negotiation skills.

# 5. DESIGN MANAGER

## Main purpose of job

To oversee the design of projects from the initial specification to the final product stage to ensure that products meet all required specifications to the required standards and satisfy customer requirements.

## Main responsibilities

1.  Oversee the design of products and test these to ensure that they meet all quality standards and specifications and satisfy customer requirements.
2.  Oversee the production of comprehensive documentation and information about products to ensure that customers are given all the required information for effective product use.
3.  Continuously review product performance and feedback from customers to develop any necessary improvements to products.
4.  Introduce and oversee a process for the research and design of new products and modifications to existing products to ensure continuous improvement.
5.  Develop and monitor the product development budget to ensure that all projects are effectively costed.
6.  Maintain a liaison with other departments to identify product needs and to produce design specifications that meet customer requirements.
7.  Research customer requirements to ensure that products meet the purposes for which they are designed and satisfy those requirements.
8.  Provide technical advice and support to other departments.

## Knowledge, skills and experience required

The job requires:

- a degree in engineering or a related discipline;
- at least 5 years' experience in the design of company products;
- significant experience in a related industry;
- project management skills;

- excellent communication skills;
- highly developed analytical and problem-solving skills;
- high-level innovation and design skills.

## 6. DEVELOPMENT ENGINEER

## Main purpose of job

To design and develop products and equipment to improve the company's product base and the performance of existing products and equipment.

## Main responsibilities

1. Design procedures to test existing products and equipment to identify areas for improvement.
2. Recommend changes to existing products and equipment to improve specifications and performance.
3. Design and develop new products and equipment to improve the company's product base.
4. Train company staff in the operation and maintenance of products and equipment.
5. Provide expert advice and assistance on technical problems relating to the modification of products and equipment.
6. Constantly monitor product testing programmes to ensure that they are delivered on time and within specification.
7. Maintain any necessary records.

## Knowledge, skills and experience required

The job requires:

- a degree-level qualification in a relevant technical discipline;
- at least 2 years' experience in the design and development of related technical products;
- knowledge of the industry sector;
- analytical skills;
- good communication skills.

# 7. DRAUGHTSPERSON

## Main purpose of job

To prepare plans, drawings, sketches and models, as required, for sites and buildings etc.

## Main responsibilities

1. Prepare plans, drawings, sketches and models as required to support design and development proposals.
2. Carry out site inspections as required to ensure the effective production of plans, drawings, sketches and models.
3. Reproduce and distribute plans, drawings etc as required.
4. Maintain all necessary records relating to plans, drawings etc.

## Knowledge, skills and experience required

The job requires:

- a technical qualification in craft design and technology;
- good technical drawing skills;
- at least 6 months' relevant experience.

## 8. ELECTRICAL ENGINEER

## Main purpose of job

To advise on all aspects of electrical power generation and transmission and to develop and monitor a programme for the electrical maintenance of plant, machinery and equipment to ensure that these continue to operate at optimum levels with a minimum of downtime.

## Main responsibilities

1. Develop preventive maintenance schedules for plant, machinery and equipment to ensure that these continue to operate at optimum levels.
2. Monitor the performance of plant and equipment to ensure that their manufacture, operation and maintenance comply with design specifications and contractual agreements.
3. Monitor and revise maintenance schedules as necessary to ensure their continued effective performance.
4. Assist in the preparation and monitoring of budgets to ensure that maintenance is carried out within agreed costs.
5. Ensure that all documentation and procedures are provided by suppliers and contractors when receiving new plant and equipment.
6. Determine the optimum level of spare parts to be held in stock to ensure that availability is maintained at minimum cost.
7. Maintain comprehensive records of stocks and maintenance carried out.
8. Maintain contact with other departments to ensure that any plant shut down is carried out at minimum cost and inconvenience.
9. Monitor the results of the planned maintenance programme and introduce any required changes where effectiveness needs to be improved.
10. Maintain knowledge of new developments in maintenance practices and procedures to ensure that there is continuous improvement in maintenance standards.

## Knowledge, skills and experience required

The job requires:

- a degree in electrical engineering;
- a chartered engineer;
- at least 3 years' experience of electrical maintenance;
- knowledge of the industry;
- good communication skills;
- good analytical and problem-solving skills;
- an ability to work as part of a team;
- knowledge of modern maintenance techniques;
- IT literacy;
- good interpersonal skills.

## 9. ELECTRICAL TECHNICIAN

## Main purpose of job

To assist in the maintenance of electrical equipment and instrumentation.

## Main responsibilities

1. Undertake routine maintenance of electrical equipment and instrumentation in accordance with the planned maintenance schedule.
2. Carry out fault finding to detect and repair any electrical faults on equipment or instrumentation.
3. Assist in producing the maintenance schedule for electrical equipment and instrumentation.
4. Supervise external contractors and internal workers as required.
5. Carry out all work within the agreed budgetary and time limits.
6. Advise other maintenance personnel on any technical issues beyond their scope.
7. Ensure that all work is carried out in accordance with company safety rules and health and safety legislation.
8. Ensure that all work is carried out in accordance with relevant environmental standards.

## Knowledge, skills and experience required

The job requires:

- HNC in electrical engineering;
- an appropriate apprenticeship or training;
- at least 5 years' experience in electrical maintenance work;
- knowledge of the industry;
- an ability to work as part of a team.

## 10. ENVIRONMENTAL MANAGER

## Main purpose of job

To ensure that the company's operations comply with the best environmental standards and relevant legislation within prescribed quality standards and costs.

## Main responsibilities

1. Undertake studies of operations and processes to ensure that these comply with the best environmental standards.
2. Review processes, techniques and equipment to determine how emissions may be reduced and compliance with environmental standards achieved.
3. Assist in the development of a strategy to ensure that the company complies with the best environmental standards and relevant legislation.
4. Maintain a relationship with the appropriate regulatory bodies to ensure that the company complies with all relevant standards and legislation.
5. Provide support and advice to other departments in the company to ensure that they are aware of their obligations in complying with environmental standards.
6. Assist in the coordination of projects to ensure that environmental issues are taken into account.
7. Maintain an up-to-date knowledge of environmental standards, legislation and relevant technology to ensure that the company complies with best practice.

## Knowledge, skills and experience required

The job requires:

- a degree or relevant technical qualification;
- at least 5 years' experience of dealing with the environmental issues arising from the operational processes involved;
- knowledge of environmental standards and relevant legislation;
- knowledge of the industry and of the processes involved;
- operational experience;
- communication skills.

# 11. FACTORY MANAGER

## Main purpose of job

To organize and control all production within the factory to achieve all output targets in terms of quantity, quality, yield, wastage, unit costs, and in accordance with health, safety and hygiene standards.

## Main responsibilities

1. Direct and control all factory staff to ensure that they are properly motivated, trained and developed, and carry out their responsibilities to the required standards and in accordance with health, safety and hygiene standards.
2. Organize all production operations to ensure that output and quality targets are achieved and that all relevant health, safety and hygiene standards are observed.
3. Develop all necessary policies and procedures to ensure that plant and equipment is effectively maintained to ensure maximum production efficiency.
4. Develop and monitor all necessary procedures to ensure the continued efficient operation and supply of services provided by utilities.
5. Develop and maintain good working relationships with customers and suppliers and organize periodic site visits to demonstrate the effectiveness of the production process.
6. Negotiate contracts with contractors and suppliers to ensure the cost-effective provision of services to the factory.
7. Develop and implement short- and long-term plans to ensure that the factory has the necessary resources to meet business objectives.
8. Develop effective working relationships with all employees and employees' representatives to ensure the maintenance of harmonious employee relations within the factory.
9. Monitor and control the factory budget to ensure that all financial and business objectives are met.

## Knowledge, skills and experience required

The job requires:

- a degree in a relevant technical subject;
- at least 10 years' production management experience;
- thorough knowledge of all aspects of the production process;
- excellent management skills;
- excellent coaching skills;
- excellent negotiating skills;
- excellent interpersonal skills;
- strong drive to achieve results.

# 12. HYGIENE OFFICER

## Main purpose of job

To ensure that all staff on the site and visitors to the site know about and observe health, safety and hygiene standards and regulations.

## Main responsibilities

1. Carry out the induction training of all staff to ensure that they are fully aware of health, safety and hygiene rules and regulations before commencing work.
2. Oversee the running of the site laundry and maintain stocks of overalls and protective clothing.
3. Negotiate contracts with external suppliers for the supply of personal protective equipment and ensure that stocks are maintained at appropriate levels.
4. Oversee all site cleaning to ensure that this is in accordance with the specified standards.
5. Carry out a regular internal audit across all parts of the site and across all shift patterns to ensure that health, safety and hygiene standards are applied, recommend any required changes and review results to ensure that recommendations are implemented.
6. Take any necessary actions and precautions to ensure effective pest control.
7. Maintain an awareness of the company's quality standards and take any necessary actions to ensure that these are adhered to.
8. Maintain an awareness of hygiene standards and introduce any required procedures and processes to ensure that these are observed by all staff.

## Knowledge, skills and experience required

The job requires:

- a technical qualification in a relevant subject;
- attendance on a recognized hygiene course;
- thorough knowledge of health, safety and hygiene standards;
- at least 1 year's experience;

- good knowledge of the plant, equipment and processes used;
- coaching skills;
- negotiating skills;
- excellent interpersonal skills.

## 13. MAINTENANCE SUPERVISOR

## Main purpose of job

To plan, organize and control all mechanical maintenance activities to ensure that all mechanical plant and equipment is maintained to the highest standards.

## Main responsibilities

1. Plan, organize and control all maintenance work within the company to ensure that plant and equipment is maintained to the required standards of quality and availability.
2. Monitor the maintenance budget to ensure that all costs are kept within the agreed limits.
3. Maintain a regular liaison with other functions to ensure that plant and equipment is available to meet operational requirements.
4. Plan a preventive maintenance schedule and ensure that all necessary maintenance is carried out at the appropriate time.
5. Supervise and train all maintenance staff to ensure that they carry out their duties effectively and maintain effective working relationships.
6. Monitor all maintenance work to ensure that it complies with all health and safety requirements.
7. Maintain accurate and up-to-date records of all plant and equipment and identify and resolve any issues relating to maintenance procedures, plant or equipment.
8. Control stock and maintain contact with the appropriate stores personnel to ensure that an adequate supply of spares and equipment is maintained.
9. Regularly review all working practices, procedures and equipment to ensure that they are the most efficient and effective available.

## Knowledge, skills and experience required

The job requires:

- at least HNC level in mechanical engineering;

- a minimum of 5 years' supervisory experience;
- experience within the industry;
- supervisory skills;
- good communication skills;
- problem-solving skills;
- planning and organizing ability;
- computer literacy;
- good interpersonal skills.

# 14. MANUFACTURING MANAGER

## Main purpose of job

To direct and control the manufacturing process to ensure that output is maintained to the required volumes and quality standards.

## Main responsibilities

1. Direct and control all manufacturing staff to ensure that they are appropriately motivated and trained and carry out their responsibilities to the required standards.
2. Oversee all manufacturing operations to ensure that they meet agreed production plans, product quality and cost standards.
3. Develop and implement any required changes to production processes to improve output and product quality and to reduce costs.
4. Identify and implement quality improvement programmes to improve the cost effectiveness of the manufacturing process.
5. Monitor all manufacturing operations and working conditions to ensure the continued provision of a safe and healthy working environment.
6. Maintain all necessary records to ensure effective monitoring of the manufacturing process.
7. Maintain an awareness of any developments in manufacturing processes to ensure that the company makes the best use of any new processes and techniques.

## Knowledge, skills and experience required

The job requires:

- a degree or relevant technical qualification in engineering discipline;
- at least 5 years' experience of manufacturing management;
- managerial experience;
- a high level of interpersonal and negotiating skills;
- thorough knowledge of the company's products and processes;
- thorough knowledge of total quality management.

# 15. MECHANICAL MAINTENANCE ENGINEER

## Main purpose of job

To develop and monitor a programme for the mechanical maintenance of plant, machinery and equipment to ensure that these continue to operate at optimum levels with a minimum of downtime.

## Main responsibilities

1. Develop preventive maintenance schedules for plant, machinery and equipment to ensure that these continue to operate at optimum levels.
2. Monitor the performance of plant and equipment and revise maintenance schedules as necessary to ensure their continued effective performance.
3. Assist in the preparation and monitoring of budgets to ensure that maintenance is carried out within agreed costs.
4. Ensure that all documentation and procedures are provided by suppliers and contractors when receiving new plant and equipment.
5. Determine the optimum level of spare parts to be held in stock to ensure that availability is maintained at minimum cost.
6. Maintain comprehensive records of stocks and maintenance carried out.
7. Maintain contact with other departments to ensure that any plant shutdown is carried out at minimum cost and inconvenience.
8. Monitor the results of the planned maintenance programme and introduce any required changes where effectiveness needs to be improved.
9. Maintain knowledge of new developments in maintenance practices and procedures to ensure that there is continuous improvement in maintenance standards.

## Knowledge, skills and experience required

The job requires:

● a degree in mechanical engineering;

- a qualification as a chartered engineer;
- at least 3 years' experience of mechanical maintenance;
- knowledge of the industry;
- good communication skills;
- good analytical and problem-solving skills;
- an ability to work as part of a team;
- knowledge of modern maintenance techniques;
- IT literacy;
- good interpersonal skills.

# 16. OPERATIONS DIRECTOR

## Main purpose of job

To direct and control all production, purchasing and distribution operations of the company to ensure that business objectives are met efficiently and effectively.

## Main responsibilities

1. Direct and control all production, purchasing and distribution employees to ensure that they are appropriately motivated and trained and carry their responsibilities to the required standards.

2. Contribute to the development of the company's corporate strategy and lead strategy development in the areas of production, purchasing and distribution to ensure that company achieves its short and long-term objectives.

3. Develop and implement all necessary policies and procedures to ensure that the production, purchasing and distribution functions achieve their business objectives.

4. Develop and control the budget for the Operations Department to ensure that the department has all the resources required to meet its objectives within agreed financial parameters.

5. Direct and control the production function to ensure that finished goods of the required standard are available to customers within agreed costs and at the right times.

6. Direct and control the purchasing function to ensure that the company has all the resources required for production purposes within agreed costs and quality standards and at the right times.

7. Direct and control the warehousing and distribution functions to ensure that customers are supplied with the right quantities of goods at the right times.

8. Develop all necessary policies and procedures to ensure that a safe and healthy working environment is maintained at all company sites.

9. Maintain an effective working relationship with all other directors to ensure that there is effective coordination of all company activities in support of corporate objectives.

10. Act as the company's main adviser on all issues relating to operational functions and keep abreast of latest developments to ensure that the company maintains its competitive position.

## Knowledge, skills and experience required

The job requires:

- a degree or equivalent and relevant professional qualifications;
- at least 10 years' experience in operations management;
- significant experience of the industry;
- significant managerial experience;
- excellent interpersonal and negotiating skills;
- thorough knowledge of the company and its products and processes;
- excellent organizational skills;
- excellent time management skills;
- excellent decision making skills.

# 17. PROCESS AUDITOR

## Main purpose of job

To review and audit all operational processes and test products and associated documentation to ensure that they are of the required quality standards, and recommend improvements where necessary.

## Main responsibilities

1. Carry out audits of all operations to ensure that they conform to established quality standards and to recommend improvements as necessary.
2. Carry out product testing to ensure that all products conform to established quality standards and recommend any necessary improvements.
3. Maintain records of all audits and reviews undertaken in accordance with laid-down standards.
4. Notify the relevant managers of any shortfall in quality standards of procedures and recommend preventive actions to ensure that company quality standards are maintained.
5. Maintain an awareness of developments in quality standards and operational processes to ensure continuous professional development and a continuing high level of service.

## Knowledge, skills and experience required

The job requires:

- HND in quality assurance;
- at least 2 years' experience of quality audit and review work;
- sound knowledge of all company products and operating processes;
- detailed knowledge of all relevant quality standards;
- good interpersonal skills;
- analytical thinking skills.

# 18. PROCESS CHEMIST

## Main purpose of job

To carry out chemical process and development work to ensure that all chemical processes, equipment and supporting systems operate to their maximum effectiveness, within specified safety and cost constraints.

## Main responsibilities

1. Assist in developing and modifying chemical processes to ensure that products are of the appropriate quality and produced within the established cost limits.
2. Monitor chemical processes to resolve any problems.
3. Undertake studies and trials of chemicals and instruments to improve production processes, unit costs, quality and safety.
4. Maintain an awareness of new developments in chemical production processes and evaluate and apply those that may be of benefit to the company.
5. Maintain an awareness of customer requirements and any complaints to identify any areas that may need development or improvement.
6. Communicate the results of research studies to managers and operators.
7. Maintain an awareness of developments in the field of chemical engineering which might have an impact on production processes.

## Knowledge, skills and experience required

The job requires:

- a degree in chemistry or chemical engineering;
- at least 3 years' experience of process engineering;
- experience within the industry;
- problem-solving skills;
- good communication skills;
- project management skills.

# 19. PROCESS ENGINEER

## Main purpose of job

To ensure that all processes, equipment and supporting systems operate to their maximum effectiveness, within specified safety and cost constraints, and that all products are of the desired quality.

## Main responsibilities

1. Develop all necessary systems and processes to ensure that products are of the appropriate quality and within the established cost limits.
2. Monitor processes to resolve any problems and remove bottlenecks.
3. Undertake studies to improve production processes, unit costs, quality and safety.
4. Maintain an awareness of new developments in technology and relevant production processes and evaluate and apply those that may be of benefit to the company.
5. Maintain an awareness of customer requirements and any complaints to identify any areas that may need development or improvement.
6. Supervise process personnel to ensure that they receive any necessary training and to resolve any production problems.

## Knowledge, skills and experience required

The job requires:

- a degree in a relevant engineering discipline;
- at least 3 years' experience of process engineering;
- experience within the industry;
- problem-solving skills;
- good communication skills;
- project management skills;
- supervisory skills.

## 20. PRODUCT TECHNICIAN

## Main purpose of job

To assemble components and products, ensuring that they meet specifications.

## Main responsibilities

1. Assemble components and products to established specifications.
2. Test components and products to ensure that they meet all requirements.
3. Address and resolve any technical problems arising in the assembly of components and products.
4. Maintain all required records of components and products assembled and any problems encountered.
5. Establish and maintain contacts with other departments to ensure that product documentation and test procedures are accurate.
6. Establish and maintain contacts with suppliers and subcontractors for technical information in relation to components and products.

## Knowledge, skills and experience required

The job requires:

- a relevant technical qualification;
- at least 1 year's experience in product assembly;
- thorough knowledge of the assembly process;
- good communication skills.

# 21. PRODUCTION ENGINEER

## Main purpose of job

To provide advice and guidance to managers and staff on the most efficient and effective engineering processes to meet production requirements.

## Main responsibilities

1. Monitor and review all engineering processes, documentation, tools, plant and computer software to ensure that these operate effectively and are appropriate to meet production targets.
2. Recommend design requirements and modifications to company products to ensure that they meet production standards and existing and future customer requirements.
3. Review and evaluate any new equipment and processes to ensure that they meet production requirements.
4. Review the engineering process and cost implications of proposed new products.
5. Recommend any necessary changes to engineering processes to improve efficiency, effectiveness and product quality.
6. Establish and maintain contacts with external suppliers to advise them of any design constraints and requirements on machinery and equipment supplied.
7. Maintain an awareness of developments in the field of production engineering to ensure that the company continues to apply the most effective processes and equipment.

## Knowledge, skills and experience required

The job requires:

- a qualification to HNC level in production engineering;
- at least 2 years' experience of production engineering in a relevant sector;
- knowledge of lean manufacturing and continuous improvement techniques;

- good knowledge of machinery and equipment used in the production process;
- good analytical skills;
- good interpersonal skills.

# 22. PRODUCTION MANAGER

## Main purpose of job

Direct and control the company's production operations to ensure that all targets are met within the specified quality standards and budgets.

## Main responsibilities

1.  Direct and control the staff of the department to ensure that they are appropriately trained and motivated and carry out their responsibilities to the required standards.
2.  Oversee all operating processes to ensure that the most efficient and effective use is made of plant and equipment and that safety standards are adhered to.
3.  Prepare and monitor budgets to ensure that the optimum use is made of production resources.
4.  Monitor output to ensure that production meets the established standards in terms of both quantity and quality.
5.  Maintain regular contact with other departments to ensure that they are aware of production requirements and to identify potential problems.
6.  Provide advice and support to other departments on production issues.
7.  Plan, introduce and monitor maintenance and work schedules to ensure that machine downtime is kept to a minimum.
8.  Maintain an awareness of new developments in production processes and propose modifications to plant and equipment so that the company makes the best use of technological developments in its sector.

## Knowledge, skills and experience required

The job requires:

*   a relevant technical or engineering qualification;
*   at least 5 years' management experience;
*   knowledge of the industry;
*   detailed knowledge of the plant, equipment and processes used;

- excellent communication skills;
- excellent interpersonal skills;
- organizing and coordinating skills.

# 23. PRODUCTION OPERATIVE

## Main purpose of job

To produce output of the quality required by the company using appropriate machinery, plant and equipment.

## Main responsibilities

1. Operate machinery and processes to produce products of the required quality.
2. Constantly monitor output to ensure that it is of the standard required, rejecting any that does not meet the standard.
3. Make any necessary adjustments to machinery or processes to ensure that the required product quality is maintained.
4. Receive and store raw materials required for the production process.
5. Monitor the use of raw materials to ensure that new supplies are ordered as required.
6. Maintain a high standard of housekeeping and ensure that all environmental and health and safety regulations are complied with.
7. Assist in the maintenance of a safe and healthy working environment and ensure that all equipment is used in accordance with safety regulations and company rules.
8. Maintain all required production records.

## Knowledge, skills and experience required

The job requires:

- a basic secondary education;
- an ability to operate relevant machinery and to comply with health and safety regulations;
- an ability to work as part of a team.

# 24. PRODUCTION PLANNER

## Main purpose of job

To advise managers and staff on the most efficient, reliable and cost-effective production schedules and engineering processes to meet production requirements.

## Main responsibilities

1. Analyse and plan production schedules, processes, documentation, tools, plant and computer software to ensure that these operate effectively and are appropriate to meet production targets.
2. Recommend modifications to production processes to ensure that production standards are maintained and improved to meet production and quality targets.
3. Review and evaluate new and existing equipment and processes to ensure that they are operating accurately and meet production requirements and standards.
4. Review the engineering process and cost implications of proposed new products.
5. Recommend any necessary changes to the layout of plant, machinery and production processes to improve efficiency, effectiveness and product quality.
6. Devise and implement inspection, testing and evaluation processes and methods for any new equipment, materials or components to ensure that they are of the required standard.
7. Maintain an awareness of developments in the field of production engineering to ensure that the company continues to apply the most effective processes and equipment.

## Knowledge, skills and experience required

The job requires:

- a qualification to HNC level in production engineering;
- at least 2 years' experience of production planning in a relevant sector;

- knowledge of lean manufacturing and continuous improvement techniques;
- excellent knowledge of product and production testing processes;
- good knowledge of machinery and equipment used in the production process;
- good analytical skills;
- good interpersonal skills.

# 25. PRODUCTION SUPERVISOR

## Main purpose of job

To supervise a team of operatives to ensure that they produce a high volume of good quality products.

## Main responsibilities

1. Supervise a team of operatives to ensure that they carry out their work effectively and safely.
2. Monitor the volume and quality of output to ensure that these are to the standards required.
3. Monitor production equipment and adjust settings as necessary to ensure that the volume and quality of output are maintained to the required standard.
4. Receive and store raw materials to ensure that there are sufficient stocks to meet production requirements.
5. Monitor manning levels on production equipment and make changes as necessary in the event of staff absence.
6. Address and resolve any technical issues arising in the production process.
7. Train operators in the production process to ensure that they work efficiently and safely.
8. Monitor the working environment to ensure that company safety policies and health and safety regulations are complied with and to provide a safe and healthy working environment.
9. Maintain all necessary production records.

## Knowledge, skills and experience required

The job requires:

- a basic secondary education;
- at least 2 years' experience in any production process;
- supervisory experience;
- an ability to carry out shift working.

# 26. PROJECT COORDINATOR

## Main purpose of job

To coordinate projects across the company to determine project objectives and timetable and to ensure that all objectives are met within agreed timescales and budgets.

## Main responsibilities

1. Maintain regular contact with operational managers and external contractors to define the scope of projects and the resulting implementation plans.
2. Define, in consultation with operational managers, the benefits, costs, key result areas and success criteria for defined projects.
3. Define project stages and the objectives and costs associated with each stage.
4. Identify the resources required at each project stage to meet project objectives and negotiate the release of these resources with operational managers.
5. Assess the impact of any one project on other concurrent projects and allocate resources as necessary to achieve the optimum results.
6. Monitor and report on project progress in a structured manner, drawing particular attention to deviations from the original project plan.
7. Maintain and update the project plan.
8. Direct and control the project team to ensure that they achieve their objectives and that the best possible use is made of available staff resources.
9. Review all projects and modify performance measures as necessary.

## Knowledge, skills and experience required

The job requires:

- educated to HNC or equivalent;
- at least 3 years' experience of large and complex business projects;
- proven skills in analysing business processes;

- thorough knowledge of project management techniques;
- excellent communication skills and an ability to communicate at all levels within the company and with external customers and suppliers;
- excellent understanding of how the different company functions and processes relate to each other;
- experience of managing interdisciplinary teams;
- experience of using project management tools;
- excellent organizational skills.

# 27. QUALITY CHECKER

## Main purpose of job

To carry out quality checks on products to ensure that they conform to the required standards.

## Main responsibilities

1. Check samples of packed products visually, by touch and by weight to ensure that they conform to requirements in terms of number, colour etc.
2. Count numbers of items in packets.
3. Check packaging to ensure that it is sound and any dates are correct.
4. Complete check sheets, summarizing checks carried out and the results.
5. Bring any problems to the attention of the supervisor.

## Knowledge, skills and experience required

The job requires:

- relevant training;
- technical knowledge of the products;
- knowledge of relevant quality standards;
- knowledge of the processes involved;
- at least 6 months' experience in manufacturing;
- a good eye for detail;
- good interpersonal skills.

# 28. QUALITY CONTROLLER

## Main purpose of job

To carry out testing of products to determine whether they are of the appropriate quality and to recommend improvements where necessary.

## Main responsibilities

1. Carry out product testing in accordance with standard procedures to ensure that products are of the required quality.
2. Maintain all necessary records of test results.
3. Identify and report on any potential improvements to products and processes.
4. Maintain an awareness of all developments in products and in test procedures.
5. Provide advice on quality issues to managers and staff.

## Knowledge, skills and experience required

The job requires:

- a relevant qualification or training at City and Guilds level or NVQ level II;
- technical knowledge of the products;
- knowledge of relevant quality standards;
- knowledge of the processes involved;
- at least 6 months' experience in manufacturing;
- a good eye for detail;
- good interpersonal skills.

# 29. QUALITY MANAGER

## Main purpose of job

To lead in the development of strategies and processes to ensure that product quality and customer satisfaction are maintained and that there is the continuous improvement of products, processes and services.

## Main responsibilities

1. Direct and control the staff of the quality department to ensure that they are well motivated and receive all necessary training and development to enable them to carry out their responsibilities to the required standards.
2. Develop strategies and processes to ensure that total quality is promoted throughout the company.
3. Develop processes and procedures to ensure that there is continuous improvement in all company operations and that waste is kept to a minimum.
4. Act as the company's expert on quality management and provide any necessary training and advice to managers and staff to ensure that they pursue the objectives of total quality management and continuous improvement.
5. Develop quality targets and measures for all company operations and monitor the performance of the company against these.
6. Provide advice and guidance to the company, its managers and staff on any regulatory aspects of total quality management.
7. Undertake all necessary research to keep abreast of developments in the fields of total quality management and continuous improvement to ensure that the company maintains its competitive position.
8. Control all departmental budgets and resources to ensure that these operate cost-effectively and in accordance with quality standards.

# Knowledge, skills and experience required

The job requires:

- a degree or relevant professional qualification;
- at least 5 years' experience of total quality management;
- significant managerial experience;
- substantial knowledge of quality improvement techniques;
- excellent interpersonal skills;
- problem-solving skills.

# 30. QUALITY SYSTEMS ANALYST

## Main purpose of job

To analyse and review all company operations and processes to ensure that they conform to established total quality standards.

## Main responsibilities

1. Monitor and review all company processes to ensure that they conform to total quality standards and that there is a process of continuous improvement.
2. Develop and implement all necessary procedures to ensure the effective monitoring of quality standards.
3. Assist in the development and maintenance of quality standards.
4. Provide any necessary training in total quality management and continuous improvement to managers and staff.
5. Provide advice and guidance to managers and staff on total quality management and continuous improvement.
6. Maintain an awareness of developments in the field of total quality management to ensure the continued provision of an effective and up-to-date service.

## Knowledge, skills and experience required

The job requires:

- qualifications to HND level in quality assurance;
- a minimum of 2 years' experience in quality management;
- a thorough knowledge of all company processes;
- computer literacy;
- problem-solving skills;
- good persuasive skills.

# 31. REPAIR TECHNICIAN

## Main purpose of job

To diagnose faults in products and carry out any necessary repairs.

## Main responsibilities

1. Diagnose faults in products and carry out repairs effectively.
2. Complete and maintain all required documentation about repairs carried out.
3. Report any product defects and suggested improvements to product development staff.
4. Maintain an awareness of all company products and development.

## Knowledge, skills and experience required

The job requires:

- a qualification equivalent to ONC or NVQ level II;
- at least 1 year's experience of fault finding and product maintenance;
- thorough knowledge of company products;
- problem-solving skills;
- an ability to read technical drawings.

# 32. SAFETY MANAGER

## Main purpose of job

To develop any necessary policies and procedures to ensure the health and safety of all employees, contractors and visitors to the company and to provide the main source of expert advice on health and safety matters to the company.

## Main responsibilities

1. Develop policies and procedures to ensure the health and safety of all employees, contractors and visitors to the company.
2. Provide the main source of advice and guidance to the company and its managers on health and safety matters.
3. Monitor the company's operations, processes and procedures to ensure that they comply with health and safety regulations.
4. Investigate and report on accidents and related incidents, recommending any changes that may be necessary, to ensure that the company complies with health and safety regulations.
5. Carry out a risk analysis for the company and recommend any changes that may be necessary.
6. Maintain good working relationships with insurers and other relevant authorities to ensure that the company's interests are safeguarded and a safe and healthy working environment is maintained.
7. Provide any necessary training to managers and staff to ensure that they comply with all health and safety requirements.
8. Review working practices and safety equipment to ensure that the company meets the requirements of insurers and other relevant bodies.
9. Maintain an awareness of developments in the field of health and safety to ensure that the company continues to comply with best practice and legal requirements.
10. Establish and maintain internal consultative processes on health and safety, particularly a safety committee.

# Knowledge, skills and experience required

The job requires:

- an engineering-related degree;
- a relevant health and safety qualification;
- at least 5 years' experience of health and safety in a similar environment;
- experience in a similar industry;
- good communication skills.

## 33. SERVICE TECHNICIAN

## Main purpose of job

To carry out repairs to company products at customer premises.

## Main responsibilities

1. Diagnose and repair faults to company products at customer's premises to their complete satisfaction.
2. Maintain records of all repairs carried out and get customer confirmation that the work was carried out to their satisfaction.
3. Give customers any necessary product information which might help them resolve minor problems and determine when a service visit is necessary.
4. Make customers aware of any new product developments to increase company sales.

## Knowledge, skills and experience required

The job requires:

- relevant technical training;
- a thorough knowledge of the company's products and components;
- technical problem-solving skills;
- an ability to relate well to customers.

# 34. SHIFT COORDINATOR

## Main purpose of job

To plan, coordinate and supervise production output within a shift to ensure that targets are met both in terms of quantity and quality and within safety parameters.

## Main responsibilities

1. Develop production plans to meet output targets in accordance with predetermined quality standards.
2. Supervise shift personnel to ensure that they carry out their responsibilities to the required standard and within safety rules and regulations.
3. Monitor output to ensure that targets have been achieved in terms of the required quality and volume.
4. Coordinate maintenance activities to ensure that there is a minimum of downtime and lost production.
5. Identify and resolve technical and personnel problems to ensure that continuous production is maintained.
6. Assist in the preparation of annual budgets.
7. Provide any necessary training and advice to shift personnel to ensure that they carry out their responsibilities effectively.
8. Continuously monitor working arrangements and procedures to ensure that the company complies with health and safety rules and environmental standards.
9. Maintain an awareness of production techniques and recommend any changes that might improve the quality or volume of output without compromising safety or environmental standards.

## Knowledge, skills and experience required

The job requires:

- a degree in an engineering discipline;
- relevant industry experience;
- at least 3 years' experience of shift management;
- problem-solving skills;
- supervisory skills;
- an ability to cope with shift working.

# 35. TECHNICAL AUTHOR

## Main purpose of job

To produce all technical documentation in support of company products and services so that customers have clear and user-friendly instructions for their use.

## Main responsibilities

1.  Research and compile information relating to company products and services to enable the preparation of accurate and up-to-date technical documentation.
2.  Prepare any required visual aids and documentation to support sales and other staff in promoting the company's products and services.
3.  Participate in the use of company products to gain practical experience of their application to ensure that technical information is accurate.
4.  Monitor feedback from customers and staff to ensure that technical documentation is clear and accurate.
5.  Train staff in the interpretation of technical documentation so that they are able to give further information to customers where required.

## Knowledge, skills and experience required

The job requires:

- a technical qualification;
- at least 2 years' experience of technical authorship;
- a thorough understanding of the company's products and services;
- written communication skills of the highest order.

## 36. TECHNICAL MANAGER

# Main purpose of job

To develop and maintain the required technical support systems, and associated advice and guidance, to enable the company to achieve its objectives.

# Main responsibilities

1.  Direct and control the staff of the department to ensure that they are appropriately motivated and trained and carry out their responsibilities to the required standards.
2.  Develop and maintain all required systems and processes to ensure that the company meets total quality standards and maintains ISO 9000 registration.
3.  Develop and oversee the implementation of all new technology, including computer software and hardware, which meets the business needs of the company's managers and staff.
4.  Develop and implement a programme of quality assessments to ensure compliance with quality standards.
5.  Provide advice and assistance to all managers and staff on technical and quality issues.
6.  Organize the provision of training to managers and staff on technical, quality and health and safety matters.
7.  Maintain full and up-to-date knowledge of all relevant technical and quality areas and associated regulations.

# Knowledge, skills and experience required

The job requires:

- a degree-level qualification in a relevant technical discipline;
- membership of a relevant professional body, eg IQA, IOSH etc;
- thorough knowledge of the technical processes involved;
- experience of managing quality and computer systems;
- knowledge of the industry;
- at least 5 years' experience in a related area;

- managerial experience;
- excellent knowledge of IT systems;
- excellent interpersonal skills.

# 37. TECHNICAL SERVICES MANAGER

## Main purpose of job

To be responsible for the technical servicing of all products supplied by the company to ensure a high level of customer satisfaction.

## Main responsibilities

1. Direct and control the staff of the department to ensure that they are appropriately motivated and trained and carry out their responsibilities to the required standards.
2. Maintain regular contact with customers to ensure that there is continuous feedback about the quality of products supplied.
3. Respond rapidly to any customer complaints so that the problem is speedily resolved to the customers' satisfaction.
4. Maintain an awareness of technical developments in the industry to ensure that the company maintains its competitive position.
5. Collect technical and other information about competitors' products to ensure that the company maintains its competitive position.
6. Arrange visits for customers and prospective customers to company sites to develop and maintain their interest in company products and services.
7. Maintain a liaison with other company staff, particularly in relation to the development of sales and marketing plans.
8. Negotiate with customers in the event of any claims against the company.

## Knowledge, skills and experience required

The job requires:

- a degree-level qualification, preferably in an engineering-related discipline;
- thorough knowledge of the technical processes involved;
- knowledge of the industry;
- at least 5 years' experience in a related area;
- managerial ability;
- excellent interpersonal and negotiating skills.

## 38. TECHNICAL SUPPORT ENGINEER

## Main purpose of job

To install company products at customer sites, train customers in the use of those products and provide after-sales support to ensure total customer satisfaction with the company's products and services.

## Main responsibilities

1. Install company products at customer sites, ensure that they are working effectively, and provide any necessary training and instruction to users.
2. Carry out the on-site repair of company products and ensure that these are working effectively.
3. Respond to technical enquiries from customers and ensure that any problems presented are resolved to their satisfaction.
4. Undertake the testing of company products and equipment, as requested, to ensure that they are working effectively.
5. Participate in a 24-hour customer support hotline to resolve any emergency inquiries.
6. Report any problems with company products to relevant company staff to ensure that these are resolved.
7. Maintain an awareness of developments in company products and those produced by competitors to ensure that the company continues to provide up-to-date and competitive products and services.

## Knowledge, skills and experience required

The job requires:

- ONC, NVQ level III or equivalent in an engineering discipline;
- a minimum of 2 years' experience of installing, maintaining and operating similar equipment;
- experience in the industry;
- computer skills;
- good interpersonal skills;
- good analytical and problem-solving skills.

# 39. WATER ENGINEER

## Main purpose of job

To research and advise on all aspects of water and hydraulic engineering, and to design and oversee the construction, operation and maintenance of engineering structures.

## Main responsibilities

1. Carry out and commission research and advise on soil mechanics, hydraulics, water and waste water treatment processes and other related engineering matters to ensure that decisions are made on the basis of the best possible information.
2. Advise on construction methods, materials, quality and safety standards to ensure that plant and equipment, working methods and processes comply with design specifications and identified standards.
3. Design water-based and hydraulic systems and structures to meet project specifications.
4. Develop preventive maintenance schedules for plant, machinery and equipment to ensure that these continue to operate at optimum levels.
5. Develop and implement control systems to monitor the performance of plant and equipment and revise maintenance schedules as necessary to ensure their continued effective performance.
6. Assist in the preparation and monitoring of budgets to ensure that maintenance is carried out within agreed costs.
7. Maintain knowledge of new developments in maintenance practices and procedures to ensure that there is continuous improvement in maintenance standards.

## Knowledge, skills and experience required

The job requires:

- a degree in water engineering;
- a chartered engineer;
- at least 3 years' experience of plant maintenance;

97

- knowledge of the industry;
- good communication skills;
- good analytical and problem-solving skills;
- an ability to work as part of a team;
- knowledge of modern maintenance techniques;
- IT literacy;
- good interpersonal skills.

# 3

# Estates and surveying

This section includes job descriptions for the following jobs:

1. Architect
2. Caretaker
3. Carpenter
4. Chief architect
5. Chief surveyor
6. Clerk of works
7. Director of estates and surveying
8. Electrician
9. Gardener
10. Maintenance manager
11. Maintenance supervisor
12. Maintenance worker
13. Painter/decorator
14. Plasterer
15. Plumber
16. Principal architect
17. Principal surveyor
18. Quantity surveyor
19. Senior surveyor
20. Surveyor

# 1. ARCHITECT

## Main purpose of job

To plan, design and supervise the construction, adaptation and development of buildings and land having regard to functional and aesthetic requirements.

## Main responsibilities

1.  Produce designs for buildings and other building projects in accordance with a brief or specification.
2.  Discuss design requirements with clients and other interested parties to determine the detailed project specification in relation to the type and style of construction, cost limitations and land-scaping and planning requirements.
3.  Carry out a thorough site survey to determine site characteristics and to assess likely problems.
4.  Advise client on details of the proposed construction, including impact on surrounding area, and keep informed of progress.
5.  Prepare detailed drawings and design specifications and submit these for approval by relevant planning authorities.
6.  Negotiate and oversee contracts with builders to ensure that work is carried out to the appropriate standards and in accordance with agreed timescales and costs.
7.  Maintain an awareness of developments in the field of architecture so that up-to-date and accurate advice can be given to clients.
8.  Monitor and audit work carried out by contractors to ensure that it is of the required standard.

## Knowledge, skills and experience required

The job requires:

- a relevant professional qualification;
- at least 3 years' post-qualification experience in architecture;
- highly developed technical drawing skills;
- negotiating skills;
- analytical skills;
- excellent interpersonal skills.

## 2. CARETAKER

## Main purpose of job

To carry out caretaking duties for a building to ensure that it is maintained to a high standard of cleanliness and security.

## Main responsibilities

1. Carry out cleaning or supervise contract cleaners to ensure that a high standard of cleanliness is maintained in the building.
2. Regularly inspect premises to ensure that they are secure, reporting any defects or work required to the appropriate manager.
3. Lock and unlock premises and set and re-set alarms as required, ensuring that a high level of security is maintained.
4. Carry out the regular servicing of sanitary, waste disposal and other hygiene equipment.
5. Carry out minor maintenance tasks on buildings, furniture, equipment and fixtures and fittings.
6. Regularly inspect all fire extinguishers and fire alarms and assist with arranging fire drills and emergency evacuation of the building.
7. Maintain First Aid facilities.
8. Assist with the monitoring and control of car parking arrangements, ensuring compliance with company procedures.

## Knowledge, skills and experience required

The job requires:

- a good basic education;
- training in caretaking;
- a basic knowledge of the law relating to health and safety as it affects buildings;
- First Aid training;
- an ability to work without close supervision;
- some practical skills.

# 3. CARPENTER

## Main purpose of job

To carry out any required carpentry work to the required standards.

## Main responsibilities

1. Examine drawings and sketches to determine work required in a particular job.
2. Carry out carpentry work as directed, including minor repairs to furniture and equipment.
3. Maintain competence in the use of drills, saws, sanders, planes, chisels and a range of other power and hand tools required for general maintenance work in carpentry and joinery.
4. Select tools appropriate for the job to be carried out.
5. Prepare lists of materials required for construction and maintenance work.
6. Select and measure cuts of wood appropriate for the work to be carried out.
7. Check accuracy of work carried out using appropriate measuring tools.
8. Maintain an awareness of all health and safety rules applying to carpentry and tools used to ensure that safe working practices are observed.
9. Maintain any required records of work carried out.

## Knowledge, skills and experience required

The job requires:

- a relevant craft qualification;
- at least 2 years' experience of carpentry and joinery;
- an ability to work as part of a team and with a minimum of supervision;
- excellent carpentry skills.

# 4. CHIEF ARCHITECT

## Main purpose of job

To direct and control architects engaged in planning, designing and supervising the construction, adaptation and development of buildings and land, having regard to functional and aesthetic requirements.

## Main responsibilities

1.  Coordinate major projects through a team to ensure that all target dates are met to the required standards and within agreed costs.
2.  Direct and control the staff of the department to ensure that they are appropriately trained and motivated and carry out their responsibilities to the required standards.
3.  Develop and monitor an annual operating budget to ensure that all financial targets are met, and regulations complied with, in relation to the function.
4.  Produce designs for more complex buildings and projects in accordance with a brief or specification.
5.  Discuss design requirements with clients and other interested parties to determine the detailed project specification in relation to the type and style of construction, cost limitations and landscaping and planning requirements.
6.  Organize or carry out a thorough site survey to determine site characteristics and to assess likely problems.
7.  Advise client on details of the proposed construction, including impact on surrounding area, and keep informed of progress.
8.  Prepare detailed drawings and design specifications and submit these for approval by relevant planning authorities.
9.  Negotiate and oversee contracts with builders and contractors to ensure that work is carried out to the appropriate standards and in accordance with agreed timescales and costs.
10. Maintain an awareness of developments in the field of architecture so that up-to-date and accurate advice can be given to clients.
11. Represent the function at external meetings with clients and potential clients to ensure that the services of the company are presented in the best light.

## Knowledge, skills and experience required

The job requires:

- a relevant professional qualification;
- at least 10 years' post-qualification experience in architecture;
- managerial skills;
- budgetary management skills;
- highly developed technical drawing skills;
- negotiating skills;
- analytical skills;
- excellent interpersonal skills.

# 5. CHIEF SURVEYOR

## Main purpose of job

To direct and control staff providing a comprehensive property surveying, engineering and maintenance service to the organization.

## Main responsibilities

1.  Direct and control all surveying staff to ensure that they are appropriately motivated and trained and carry out their responsibilities to the required standards.
2.  Advise managers and staff of the organization on all matters relating to building maintenance and modernization to ensure that properties are maintained to the required standards.
3.  Review the feasibility of proposed programmes of works and make recommendations about implementation and costs.
4.  Coordinate more complex projects to ensure that they are achieved within budgetary and time constraints and in accordance with regulations.
5.  Develop and monitor an annual operating budget to ensure that all financial targets are met, and regulations complied with, in relation to the surveying function.
6.  Oversee the preparation of tender documentation, including the compilation of schedules of rates, schedules of works, designs, drawings, conditions of contracts, specifications etc, and make recommendations on tenders received.
7.  Supervise the implementation of contracts for the maintenance and modernization of buildings to ensure that work is carried out to the required standards and within agreed budgets and time-scales.
8.  Represent the organization at courts or tribunal proceedings on matters relating to land and property to ensure that the organization's interests are safeguarded.
9.  Maintain an awareness of developments in the field of surveying to ensure the provision of comprehensive and accurate advice in this area.

## Knowledge, skills and experience required

The job requires:

- a relevant professional qualification;
- at least 10 years' post-qualification experience in the field of surveying;
- managerial experience;
- organizational skills;
- analytical skills;
- excellent interpersonal skills.

# 6. CLERK OF WORKS

## Main purpose of job

To represent architects on building projects to ensure compliance with design specifications and material and construction standards.

## Main responsibilities

1. Agree the programme of building work with contractors and engineers to ensure that there is complete understanding about what is required.
2. Regularly inspect work in progress to ensure compliance with design specifications and required material and construction standards.
3. Maintain records of all excavations, foundations and other work that will be hidden by subsequent construction.
4. Maintain regular contact with architect to report on progress and standards of building work carried out.
5. Instruct contractors about any remedial work that may be required and advise on any design problems.
6. Record details of all agreed deviations from contract.

## Knowledge, skills and experience required

The job requires:

- a relevant technical qualification;
- at least 3 years' experience of building construction;
- excellent negotiating skills;
- good interpersonal skills;
- good decision-making skills.

## 7. DIRECTOR OF ESTATES AND SURVEYING

## Main purpose of job

To direct and control the estates and surveying department to ensure the most effective use and maintenance of the company's properties.

## Main responsibilities

1. Direct and control the staff of the department to ensure that they are appropriately motivated and trained to enable them to carry out their responsibilities to the required standards.
2. Contribute to the development of the company's strategic plan, particularly in relation to the effective use of the company's properties.
3. Develop and monitor an annual operating budget to ensure that all financial targets are met, and regulations complied with, in relation to estates management.
4. Negotiate service level agreements with internal customers, ensuring that all agreed targets are met to the standards agreed.
5. Develop and monitor an accommodation strategy for the company to ensure that properties are used to their maximum effectiveness.
6. Oversee the maintenance of the company's properties to ensure that they are of the required standard.
7. Develop, implement and maintain all necessary health and safety systems, procedures and practices to ensure a safe, healthy and pleasant working environment.
8. Develop and maintain any necessary purchasing systems and procedures to enable the company to purchase at competitive prices any goods and materials required to maintain its properties to a high standard.
9. Act as the company's principal adviser on matters relating to estates and surveying.
10. Commission any necessary work required to maintain properties to the standards required, conforming to agreed procedures, and monitor any such work to ensure that it is carried out to the required standard and within the agreed budget.

11.   Negotiate contracts with external contractors to carry out major capital projects and minor works, ensuring the best value for money for the company.

## Knowledge, skills and experience required

The job requires:

- a degree and relevant professional qualification;
- at least 10 years' experience in a senior estates management or surveying role;
- substantial management experience;
- facilities management experience;
- experience of managing budgets;
- thorough knowledge of health and safety legislation;
- negotiating skills;
- project management skills;
- planning and organizing skills;
- excellent interpersonal skills.

# 8. ELECTRICIAN

## Main purpose of job

To carry out any required electrical work to the required standard.

## Main responsibilities

1. Examine drawings, wiring diagrams and sketches to determine work required on a particular job.
2. Carry out electrical work as directed, including the testing and repair of all electrical equipment.
3. Maintain competence in the use of power and hand tools and electrical testing equipment required for general electrical maintenance work.
4. Select tools and equipment appropriate to the job to be carried out.
5. Maintain an awareness of all relevant IEEE and Electricity at Work regulations and health and safety rules applying to electrical work to ensure that safe working practices are observed.
6. Maintain any required records of work carried out.

## Knowledge, skills and experience required

The job requires:

- a relevant craft qualification;
- at least 5 years' experience of electrical work;
- an ability to work as part of a team and with a minimum of supervision;
- electrical fault finding skills.

# 9. GARDENER

## Main purpose of job

To carry out any required gardening and horticultural work to the required standard.

## Main responsibilities

1. Prepare ground for planting and install drainage systems as necessary.
2. Grow, plant and transplant seeds, bulbs, tubers etc.
3. Carry out regular maintenance of plants and gardens through pruning, weeding, digging, fertilizing etc to ensure optimum plant growth.
4. Carry out any necessary disease and pest control activities to protect plant growth.
5. Cut and lay turf and maintain lawns through mowing, rolling, watering and feeding.
6. Construct and maintain garden features such as paths, rockeries, ponds, sheds etc.
7. Maintain competence in the use of all tools required for general gardening work.
8. Prepare lists of materials required for gardening work.
9. Maintain an awareness of all health and safety rules applying to all gardening work and tools and equipment used to ensure that safe working practices are observed.
10. Maintain any required records of work carried out.

## Knowledge, skills and experience required

The job requires:

- a relevant craft qualification;
- good horticultural knowledge;
- at least 2 years' experience of gardening;
- an ability to work as part of a team and with a minimum of supervision;
- commitment to producing work of a high standard.

# 10. MAINTENANCE MANAGER

## Main purpose of job

To plan and organize the maintenance and improvement of the company's properties to ensure that buildings and services are of the required standard and provide a safe and healthy working environment.

## Main responsibilities

1.  Direct and control all maintenance staff to ensure that they are appropriately motivated and trained and carry out their responsibilities to the required standards.
2.  Prepare specifications, obtain tenders and negotiate contracts for maintenance and minor works, ensuring that work is undertaken to the required standards and within agreed timescales and costs.
3.  Monitor the maintenance budget to ensure that this is appropriately allocated and so that the company achieves the best value for money.
4.  Develop and implement a planned maintenance programme to ensure that buildings and services are maintained to the required standards.
5.  Develop and maintain all necessary systems and procedures to ensure the safety and security of buildings and services.
6.  Provide technical advice on maintenance issues to managers and staff.
7.  Monitor all buildings and services to ensure that they conform to health and safety standards and ensure that contractors are made aware of these requirements.
8.  Develop, implement and maintain any necessary systems and procedures to ensure effective energy management within the company.

## Knowledge, skills and experience required

The job requires:

- an appropriate professional or technical qualification;
- at least 10 years' experience in building maintenance;
- good knowledge of building regulations and relevant health and safety legislation;
- extensive managerial experience;
- project management experience;
- an ability to manage contractors;
- good negotiating skills;
- good planning and organizing skills;
- excellent interpersonal skills.

# 11. MAINTENANCE SUPERVISOR

## Main purpose of job

To supervise staff involved in all aspects of maintaining the company's buildings, sites and services to ensure the safe and uninterrupted continuation of the company's activities and operations.

## Main responsibilities

1. Supervise staff to ensure that they are appropriately trained and motivated and so that they carry out their responsibilities to the standards required.
2. Assist with the development of a planned maintenance programme to ensure that sites and services continue operation without interruption and to the required standards.
3. Oversee various buildings and works projects, ensuring that work is undertaken to the standards required and within budget and timescale.
4. Maintain contact with contractors to ensure that they carry out their work to the required standards and so that they are kept aware of the company's safety policies and procedures.
5. Maintain all necessary financial records relating to contracts to ensure that payments are made at the appropriate time.
6. Provide technical advice and support to managers and staff on all matters relating to the repair and maintenance of buildings.
7. Maintain all necessary records of maintenance work carried out.

## Knowledge, skills and experience required

The job requires:

- a technical qualification equivalent to HNC;
- at least 5 years' practical experience in building maintenance;
- good knowledge of building regulations, construction regulations, fire regulations, and health and safety regulations in general;
- experience of managing staff;
- experience of dealing with contractors;

- good negotiating skills;
- excellent time and management skills;
- problem-solving skills;
- excellent communication skills.

# 12. MAINTENANCE WORKER

(See also 'office maintenance worker' in the administration job descriptions)

## Main purpose of job

To carry out any general maintenance work not requiring a skilled craftsman.

## Main responsibilities

1. Assist craftsmen in carrying out a range of maintenance work, including minor electrical, plumbing, decorating, gardening and carpentry work.
2. Carry out minor repairs to buildings, furniture, equipment, fixtures and fittings.
3. Carry out general grounds maintenance and gardening work.
4. Assist with porterage and the movement and setting up of furniture and equipment.
5. Maintain competence in the use of power and hand tools required for general maintenance work.
6. Select tools and materials appropriate to the job to be carried out.
7. Prepare lists of materials and items required for carrying out minor repairs and maintenance.
8. Maintain an awareness of all health and safety rules applying to all general maintenance work and tools used to ensure that safe working practices are observed.
9. Maintain any required records of work carried out and report any defects in buildings, furniture and equipment.

## Knowledge, skills and experience required

The job requires:

- a basic level of education;
- good all-round practical skills;
- at least 1 year's experience of carrying out general maintenance work;
- an ability to work as part of a team and with a minimum of supervision.

# 13. PAINTER/DECORATOR

## Main purpose of job

To carry out any required painting and decorating work to the required standard.

## Main responsibilities

1. Erect platforms and scaffolding for access to work, in accordance with health and safety guidelines.
2. Prepare and clean surfaces prior to painting or decoration.
3. Apply primer, undercoat and finishing coats using a variety of brushes, rollers or sprays.
4. Measure and apply wallpaper and wall coverings, matching patterns as required and ensuring that the final finish is to the required standard.
5. Design and produce decorative effects and designs as required.
6. Maintain competence in the use of all tools required for general painting and decorating work.
7. Prepare lists of materials required for painting and decorating work.
8. Maintain an awareness of all health and safety rules applying to all painting and decorating work and tools and equipment used to ensure that safe working practices are observed.
9. Maintain any required records of work carried out.

## Knowledge, skills and experience required

The job requires:

- a relevant craft qualification;
- at least 5 years' experience of painting and decorating;
- an ability to work as part of a team and with a minimum of supervision;
- commitment to producing work of a high standard.

# 14. PLASTERER

## Main purpose of job

To carry out any required plastering work to the required standard.

## Main responsibilities

1. Make plaster to the required consistency and apply to surface using any necessary tools to produce required finish.
2. Produce ornamental mouldings from casts.
3. Measure, cut and install plasterboard and ornamental plasterwork on both walls and ceilings.
4. Check finish to ensure that all services are level and joints are sealed.
5. Maintain competence in the use of power and hand tools required for general plastering work.
6. Prepare lists of materials required for plastering work.
7. Maintain an awareness of all health and safety rules applying to all plastering work and tools used to ensure that safe working practices are observed.
8. Maintain any required records of work carried out.

## Knowledge, skills and experience required

The job requires:

- a relevant craft qualification;
- at least 5 years' experience of plastering;
- an ability to work as part of a team and with a minimum of supervision;
- commitment to producing work of a high standard.

## 15. PLUMBER

## Main purpose of job

To carry out any required plumbing work to the required standard.

## Main responsibilities

1.  Examine drawings and sketches to determine work required in a particular job.
2.  Carry out plumbing and drainage work as directed, including the repair and upgrading of existing services and the installation of minor works, to ensure that all sanitary arrangements conform to health and hygiene standards, and relevant statutes, bye-laws and regulations.
3.  Maintain competence in the use of power and hand tools required for general maintenance work in plumbing and drainage.
4.  Select tools and materials appropriate to the job to be carried out.
5.  Prepare lists of materials required for plumbing and drainage work.
6.  Select, measure and cut pipes and select fittings appropriate to the work to be carried out.
7.  Test work carried out to ensure effective operation.
8.  Maintain an awareness of all health and safety rules applying to all plumbing and drainage work and tools used to ensure that safe working practices are observed.
9.  Maintain any required records of work carried out.

## Knowledge, skills and experience required

The job requires:

- a relevant craft qualification;
- at least 5 years' experience of plumbing and drainage work;
- an ability to work as part of a team and with a minimum of supervision;
- fault finding skills.

# 16. PRINCIPAL ARCHITECT

## Main purpose of job

To supervise a team of architects engaged in planning, designing and supervising the construction, adaptation and development of buildings and land having regard to functional and aesthetic requirements.

## Main responsibilities

1.  Coordinate major projects through a team to ensure that all target dates are met to the required standards and within agreed costs.
2.  Supervise the team to ensure that they are appropriately trained and motivated and carry out their responsibilities to the required standards.
3.  Produce designs for more complex buildings and projects in accordance with a brief or specification.
4.  Discuss design requirements with clients and other interested parties to determine the detailed project specification in relation to the type and style of construction, cost limitations and landscaping and planning requirements.
5.  Commission or carry out a thorough site survey to determine site characteristics and to assess likely problems.
6.  Advise client on details of the proposed construction, including impact on surrounding area, and keep informed of progress.
7.  Prepare detailed drawings and design specifications and submit these for approval by relevant planning authorities.
8.  Negotiate and oversee contracts with builders to ensure that work is carried out to the appropriate standards and in accordance with agreed timescales and costs.
9.  Maintain an awareness of developments in the field of architecture so that up-to-date and accurate advice can be given to clients.
10. Monitor and audit work carried out by contractors to ensure that it is of the required standard.

# Knowledge, skills and experience required

The job requires:

- a relevant professional qualification;
- at least 5 years' post-qualification experience in architecture;
- managerial skills;
- highly developed technical drawing skills;
- negotiating skills;
- analytical skills;
- excellent interpersonal skills.

# 17. PRINCIPAL SURVEYOR

## Main purpose of job

To direct and control staff providing a comprehensive property surveying, engineering and maintenance service to the organization.

## Main responsibilities

1. Direct and control a team of surveying staff to ensure that they are appropriately motivated and trained and carry out their responsibilities to the required standards.
2. Advise managers and staff of the organization on all matters relating to building maintenance and modernization to ensure that properties are maintained to the required standards.
3. Devise and implement maintenance and modernization programmes to ensure that properties are maintained to the required standards.
4. Implement and monitor approved maintenance and modernization programmes to ensure that work is carried out to the required standards and within agreed budgets and timescales.
5. Oversee the preparation of tender documentation, including the compilation of schedules of rates, schedules of works, designs, drawings, conditions of contracts, specifications etc, and make recommendations on tenders received.
6. Supervise the implementation of contracts for the maintenance and modernization of buildings to ensure that work is carried out to the required standards and within agreed budgets and timescales.
7. Represent the organization at courts or tribunal proceedings on matters relating to land and property to ensure that the organization's interests are safeguarded.
8. Maintain an awareness of developments in the field of surveying and property maintenance to ensure the provision of comprehensive and accurate advice in these areas.

# Knowledge, skills and experience required

The job requires:

- a relevant professional qualification;
- at least 5 years' post-qualification experience in the field of surveying and building maintenance;
- managerial experience;
- organizational skills;
- analytical skills;
- excellent interpersonal skills.

# 18. QUANTITY SURVEYOR

## Main purpose of job

To advise on financial and contractual issues relating to bills of quantities provided in relation to material supplied for construction projects.

## Main responsibilities

1. Draw up contracts specifying nature and quantity of raw materials required.
2. Review tenders received and advise client on which to accept.
3. Draw up detailed cost plans and advise contractors and engineers on the limits they must work to in terms of quantity and quality.
4. Keep client informed of project costs and discuss and agree any proposed variation.
5. Measure and value work in progress to ensure that it is within the agreed parameters.
6. Measure and value completed project and authorize payment provided the contract is within the agreed specifications.
7. Maintain an awareness of developments in the field of quantity surveying and up-to-date knowledge of costs of construction materials to ensure that advice is reliable.

## Knowledge, skills and experience required

The job requires:

- a relevant technical qualification;
- at least 2 years' post-qualification experience in the field of quantity surveying;
- excellent knowledge of construction materials;
- negotiating skills;
- good interpersonal skills.

# 19. SENIOR SURVEYOR

## Main purpose of job

To assist in providing a comprehensive property surveying, engineering and maintenance service to the organization.

## Main responsibilities

1. Carry out a programme of regular inspection of properties, and a number of random checks, to report on any matters requiring attention.
2. Advise managers and staff of the organization on matters relating to building maintenance and modernization to ensure that properties are maintained to the required standards.
3. Implement and monitor approved maintenance and modernization programmes to ensure that work is carried out to the required standards and within agreed budgets and timescales.
4. Prepare tender documentation, including the compilation of schedules of rates, schedules of works, designs, drawings, conditions of contracts, specifications etc, and make recommendations on tenders received.
5. Supervise the implementation of contracts for the maintenance and modernization of buildings to ensure that work is carried out to the required standards and within agreed budgets and timescales.
6. Maintain an awareness of developments in the field of surveying and property maintenance to ensure the provision of comprehensive and accurate advice in these areas.

## Knowledge, skills and experience required

The job requires:

- a relevant professional qualification;
- at least 3 years' post-qualification experience in the field of surveying and building maintenance;
- supervisory experience;
- organizational skills;
- analytical skills;
- excellent interpersonal skills.

# 20. SURVEYOR

## Main purpose of job

To carry out surveys of property and sites to provide information for building construction, alterations, valuations, land use and map making.

## Main responsibilities

1.  Survey, measure and inspect properties and sites to establish property boundaries and to provide information for construction projects.
2.  Inspect properties on a regular basis to determine need for alterations and repairs.
3.  Advise clients and managers and staff of the organization on matters relating to building maintenance and repair to ensure that properties are maintained to the required standards.
4.  Monitor approved maintenance and modernization programmes to ensure that work is carried out to the required standards and within agreed budgets and timescales.
5.  Supervise the implementation of contracts for the maintenance and modernization of buildings to ensure that work is carried out to the required standards and within agreed budgets and timescales.
6.  Maintain an awareness of developments in the field of surveying to ensure the continued provision of comprehensive and accurate advice in this area.

## Knowledge, skills and experience required

The job requires:

* a relevant technical qualification;
* at least 2 years' post-qualification experience in the field of surveying and building maintenance;
* analytical skills;
* good interpersonal skills.

# 4

# Finance and accountancy

This section includes job descriptions for the following jobs:

1. Accounts clerk
2. Accounts clerk – controls and reconciliations
3. Accounts supervisor
4. Actuary
5. Auditor
6. Cashier
7. Chief internal auditor
8. Credit controller
9. Credit manager
10. Director of finance and information systems
11. Finance director
12. Financial accountant
13. Financial controller
14. Management accountant
15. Payroll assistant
16. Payroll supervisor
17. Principal accountant/section head
18. Sales ledger clerk

19. Senior accountant
20. Senior internal auditor
21. Systems accountant

# 1. ACCOUNTS CLERK

## Main purpose of job

To undertake routine clerical duties in support of the accountancy function.

## Main responsibilities

1. Process payments and invoices accurately and in accordance with closely defined procedures and timescales.
2. Verify calculations and input computer codes for a variety of documents.
3. Check ledgers, statements and accounts to identify errors and take any necessary corrective action, referring more complex items to the supervisor.
4. Respond to customer enquiries and complaints, by telephone or in writing, after having checked the relevant facts from existing records.
5. Carry out any statistical analysis and produce reports as required.
6. Draft any routine correspondence.
7. Undertake routine administrative support procedures, such as assisting with filing, opening post etc.
8. Prepare cheques for payment.
9. Maintain accurate financial records, including data input to the computer.

## Knowledge, skills and experience required

The job requires:

- qualifications to GCSE level, including English and Maths;
- previous experience in an accounts office;
- an understanding of office procedures;
- accuracy;
- computer and keyboard skills;
- a good telephone manner.

# 2. ACCOUNTS CLERK – CONTROLS AND RECONCILIATIONS

## Main purpose of job

To assist in providing support in all aspects of financial control and reconciliations.

## Main responsibilities

1. Provide support in the development of all necessary financial controls and in carrying out reconciliations to ensure the production of accurate financial records and information.
2. Carry out reconciliations of balance sheet accounts to ensure that all accounting records are accurate.
3. Input data into the computer and produce reports for management information and for completion of returns required by statute and other regulations.
4. Prepare monthly management accounts to produce timely and accurate management information.
5. Assist in preparing the annual budget.
6. Maintain ledgers as required.

## Knowledge, skills and experience required

The job requires:

- qualifications to GCSE level, including English and Maths;
- ideally studying for an accountancy qualification or qualified to accounting technician level;
- knowledge of accounting systems;
- accuracy;
- an ability to understand and use computerized spreadsheet packages;
- a good telephone manner.

# 3. ACCOUNTS SUPERVISOR

## Main purpose of job

To carry out general financial accounting and administrative duties in relation to accounts payable and purchases, to help the company achieve its financial and business objectives.

## Main responsibilities

1. Supervise the staff of the section to ensure that all required training and development is received and that work is carried out to the required standards.
2. Oversee the day-to-day operations of the purchase ledger.
3. Maintain the process for payment of accounts to ensure that the company meets its obligations as they fall due, complies with its payment policy and secures discounts where applicable.
4. Assist with the implementation of travel and subsistence policies and procedures, keeping policies in line with tax legislation, ensuring compliance with policy, and ensuring that the company obtains best value from its travel arrangements.
5. Act as the main budget contact for specific departments, assisting with the setting and monitoring of those budgets and providing all other advice and assistance those budget holders require.
6. Promote and build good working relationships with all parts of the company, providing advice and assistance to all staff on any aspect of financial or accounting processes and procedures.
7. Assist with the effective and timely preparation of budgets, annual financial accounts, management accounts, and cash flow forecasts as required.
8. Supervise the petty cash system.
9. Keep systems and procedures under constant review to ensure that they continue to contribute to the provision of a high quality service to the company.

# Knowledge, skills and experience required

The job requires:

- accountancy qualifications to Accounting Technician level;
- considerable experience of working in accounts with a minimum of 3 years, ideally in a similar environment;
- experience of staff supervision;
- good interpersonal and communication skills;
- accuracy.

# 4. ACTUARY

## Main purpose of job

To analyse and interpret data using economic, statistical and actuarial principles and techniques to assist in management decision making and with the formulation of financial and investment policies.

## Main responsibilities

1. Decide what data is required for any particular project and determine the most appropriate methods for the collection and analysis of this data.
2. Analyse and interpret data using statistical, financial, economic and other appropriate techniques and advise managers on the appropriate actions and policies to be pursued in the light of these findings.
3. Prepare and present reports, charts, and tables summarizing findings and recommendations.
4. Establish and maintain regular contact with relevant departments and employees in the company to gather relevant data.
5. Maintain an awareness of developments in the actuarial field to ensure that the latest techniques and approaches are applied.

## Knowledge, skills and experience required

The job requires:

- qualification to degree level;
- a relevant professional qualification;
- at least 5 years' experience of actuarial analysis;
- a high level of competence in mathematical, statistical and economic analysis;
- a high level of accuracy;
- good report-writing and presentation skills;
- good interpersonal skills.

# 5. AUDITOR

## Main purpose of job

To review and evaluate control systems and procedures to ensure that management policies are being complied with, assets are safeguarded, information is maintained in a secure and accurate manner and legal requirements are complied with.

## Main responsibilities

1. Review and evaluate internal procedures and supporting documentation to ensure that they provide an effective control system and to identify any weaknesses.
2. Carry out audits and compliance testing to ensure that procedures are operating effectively with appropriate controls and recommend changes where necessary.
3. Provide information and assistance to managers and staff to enable them to comply with financial and statutory requirements.
4. Carry out reviews of specific functions and processes to promote best value and recommend improvements.
5. Assist in the development of any internal audit programme to ensure that all functions are subject to systematic review.
6. Assist in the development and maintenance of new systems and procedures to assist managers and staff in complying with financial regulations and meeting their objectives.

## Knowledge, skills and experience required

The job requires:

- qualification to accountancy technician standard;
- at least 2 years' experience of internal audit;
- general accountancy experience;
- excellent computer skills;
- excellent analytical skills;
- accuracy;
- good interpersonal skills.

## 6. CASHIER

## Main purpose of job

To collect and process cash payments using manual and/or computerized accountancy processes.

## Main responsibilities

1. Collect, account for and bank cash received and issue receipts using a computerized cash receipting process.
2. Maintain accurate financial records of cash collected, carrying out regular balances of cash transactions and resolving any discrepancies.
3. Reconcile cash transactions to general ledgers and bank statements.
4. Provide information to customers in response to a wide variety of enquiries and complaints to ensure that they receive the best possible customer service.
5. Maintain all necessary records and information in a secure and accurate manner to ensure that there is full information about cash transactions.
6. Maintain regular contact with internal accounting staff and banks to receive and pass on relevant information.
7. Take all necessary security precautions to ensure that cash is held in a safe and secure manner.

## Knowledge, skills and experience required

The job requires:

- education to GCSE level;
- at least 1 year's experience as a cashier;
- good knowledge of bookkeeping and of the procedures for processing payments and receipts;
- good keyboard skills and computer literacy;
- numeracy and accuracy;
- good interpersonal and communication skills.

# 7. CHIEF INTERNAL AUDITOR

## Main purpose of job

To direct and control the internal audit function, ensuring that all financial standards, regulations, and statutory provisions are complied with and that there are the appropriate financial controls to ensure the efficient, effective and proper use of resources.

## Main responsibilities

1. Direct and control all internal audit staff to ensure that they are appropriately motivated and trained and carry out their responsibilities to the required standards.
2. Develop and implement an annual audit plan to ensure that the organization complies with financial and statutory regulations and standards.
3. Monitor the conduct of internal audits to ensure that all relevant activities are subject to periodic audit.
4. Present audit reports to the Board and committees to identify areas requiring attention and ensure implementation of any actions agreed.
5. Develop all necessary internal controls to ensure that financial systems operate effectively and to identify potential problems.
6. Maintain a working relationship with external auditors to ensure that they have all the information they might require.
7. Carry out ad hoc audit reviews to investigate any areas identified by management.

## Knowledge, skills and experience required

The job requires:

- qualification as a chartered accountant or auditor;
- at least 5 years' post-qualification experience of auditing and accountancy;
- significant management experience;
- detailed knowledge of financial and audit standards, regulations and requirements;

- good knowledge of the organization;
- analytical skills;
- report writing and presentation skills.

# 8. CREDIT CONTROLLER

## Main purpose of job

To maintain the debtors ledger accurately and to ensure that all income due is received and accurately accounted for.

## Main responsibilities

1. Maintain the debtors ledger to ensure that all balances are correct.
2. Monitor any outstanding invoices and process these to ensure that they are paid as soon as possible.
3. Respond to customer enquiries to ensure that any queries are resolved to the customer's satisfaction.
4. Consult sales staff to ensure that any disputes about deliveries and payments are resolved.
5. Set up new accounts as required.

## Knowledge, skills and experience required

The job requires:

- education to GCSE level;
- credit control experience;
- good numeracy skills;
- good telephone manner;
- ability to use spreadsheets.

# 9. CREDIT MANAGER

## Main purpose of job

To provide a comprehensive credit control service to the company so that the potential for bad debts is minimized.

## Main responsibilities

1. Direct and control the credit control team to ensure that they are appropriately motivated and trained and carry out their responsibilities to the required standards.
2. Authorize new accounts following any necessary status checks to ensure that customers have the necessary resources to meet their commitments.
3. Review existing accounts to determine the current credit position of customers and to ensure that they are able to meet their commitments to the company.
4. Monitor all overdue accounts and take any necessary action to ensure that these are collected in accordance with the company's credit policies.
5. Take all necessary action to recover payments where customers are in default.
6. Investigate any complaints by customers that might result in them disputing invoices or withholding payments.
7. Take all necessary actions to withdraw credit facilities from customers who default on payments.
8. Write off any bad debts where customers have gone into bankruptcy or liquidation or where the cost of pursuing the debt is uneconomic.
9. Maintain all necessary records and ensure that relevant financial information is passed to accountancy staff.

## Knowledge, skills and experience required

The job requires:

- professional membership of the Institute of Credit Management;
- managerial experience;

- at least 2 years' credit control experience;
- computer literacy;
- good understanding of financial accounts;
- good interpersonal skills.

# 10. DIRECTOR OF FINANCE AND INFORMATION SYSTEMS

## Main purpose of job

To direct and control the staff of the department to ensure that the company's financial and IS targets are met as efficiently and effectively as possible and to contribute to the development of the company's strategic objectives.

## Main responsibilities

1. Direct and control the staff of the Finance and Information Systems Department to ensure that they are appropriately motivated and trained and carry out their responsibilities to the required standards.
2. Contribute to the development of the company's corporate strategy and develop and implement the financial and IS strategies to ensure the attainment and delivery of plans and objectives.
3. Provide information and advice on financial management, financial control and procedures, and information systems, to the Board, directors and staff to ensure that the company's mission and financial and IS objectives are met.
4. Prepare and implement an annual budget and regular updates to ensure the sound management of the company's finances and to ensure that financial objectives are met.
5. Develop and maintain all necessary financial and IS systems and procedures to ensure the effective and efficient attainment of corporate objectives.
6. Develop, control and implement a programme of internal audit to ensure that company operations are carried out efficiently and with probity and that agreed recommendations are implemented.
7. Maintain a close working relationship with the external auditors to ensure compliance and cooperation with their requirements and to provide an effective audit trail.
8. Negotiate and control all financial and IS contracts to ensure that services provide optimum value to the company.

9.  Develop and maintain appropriate arrangements for effective cash management, making payments, collecting receipts, securing banking arrangements, monitoring income and ensuring optimum value to the company.
10. Recommend and implement arrangements for costing and appraising all proposals with resource implications, including those relating to the use of external contractors and consultants, and recommend appropriate qualitative and quantitative performance measures.
11. Devise and implement appropriate financial and administrative procedures for the company and ensure that these operate effectively and are communicated to all staff.

## Knowledge, skills and experience required

The job requires:

- a qualified accountant;
- thorough knowledge of IT systems;
- at least 10 years' accountancy experience at a senior level;
- senior-level managerial experience;
- excellent interpersonal skills;
- problem-solving skills;
- decision-making skills.

# 11. FINANCE DIRECTOR

## Main purpose of job

To contribute to the attainment of the company's business objectives by:

(a)  providing strategic and financial guidance to ensure that the company's financial commitments are met; and

(b)  developing all necessary policies and procedures to ensure the sound financial management and control of the company's business.

## Main responsibilities

1.  Direct and control finance staff to ensure that they are appropriately motivated and developed and so that they carry out their responsibilities to the required standards.

2.  Contribute to the achievement of the company's business objectives by providing advice and guidance on financial strategy.

3.  Develop and control the company's annual operating budget to ensure that all financial targets are met and financial and statutory regulations complied with.

4.  Provide financial advice and guidance to the company's managers and staff to enable them to achieve their objectives.

5.  Oversee the preparation of the company's financial accounts to ensure that these are presented accurately and on time.

6.  Develop and implement an internal audit programme to ensure that the company complies with financial procedures and regulations.

7.  Develop and maintain all necessary systems, policies and procedures to ensure effective and efficient financial management within the company.

8.  Monitor external contracts and services provided by suppliers to ensure that these are operating effectively and provide the best value to the company.

9.  Carry out all necessary actions to ensure that the company meets its financial and legal obligations.

## Knowledge, skills and experience required

The job requires:

- qualification as a chartered accountant;
- a minimum of 10 years' senior-level accountancy experience;
- significant managerial experience;
- knowledge of the industry;
- strategic thinking skills;
- excellent interpersonal skills.

## 12. FINANCIAL ACCOUNTANT

## Main purpose of job

To develop and implement financial policies for the company to ensure the effective financial management of the company's affairs and compliance with any relevant regulations.

## Main responsibilities

1. Develop and implement all necessary financial policies and procedures to ensure the provision of an effective financial management service and compliance with any relevant regulations.
2. Maintain reliable and accurate accounting records for the company and produce management accounts as necessary to facilitate the effective management of the company.
3. Assist in the preparation of the annual budget and produce cash flow forecasts and variances against budget projections to assist decision making.
4. Maintain day-to-day control of all accounting systems to ensure the complete and accurate processing of financial data in accordance with internal procedures.
5. Produce regular analyses of income and expenditure to assist managers in the budget monitoring process.
6. Supervise accountancy staff to ensure that they are appropriately motivated and trained and carry out their responsibilities effectively.
7. Assist in the development, review and improvement of accountancy and computer systems within the company.
8. Provide advice on financial accountancy issues to managers and staff as required.

## Knowledge, skills and experience required

The job requires:

- an accountancy qualification;
- a minimum of 2 years' experience of preparing management accounts, budgets and cash flow forecasts;

- experience of computerized accounting packages;
- experience of supervising staff;
- ability to analyse complex financial information and produce reports;
- good interpersonal skills.

# 13. FINANCIAL CONTROLLER

## Main purpose of job

To develop and maintain all necessary financial controls, systems and processes to ensure the efficient and effective management of the company's finances and compliance with statutory requirements.

## Main responsibilities

1.  Develop systems and procedures to ensure the efficient and effective management of the company's finances and compliance with statutory requirements.
2.  Direct and control Finance staff to ensure that they are appropriately motivated and trained and carry out their responsibilities to the required standards.
3.  Produce accurate and timely financial information about the company's financial status and performance to enable decisions to be taken relating to the company's financial strength and security.
4.  Produce all necessary statements and reports to enable the accurate measurement of cash flow, profit and loss, stock and debtors etc.
5.  Develop and monitor all necessary controls to ensure that the company complies with statutory requirements.
6.  Act as the main point of contact with external auditors and provide them with all required information.
7.  Carry out any necessary internal audit reviews and monitor the financial effectiveness of systems and controls.
8.  Recommend any changes necessary to improve the company's financial performance and financial controls.
9.  Keep up to date with any developments in financial management which might affect how the company's finances are managed or its statutory obligations.
10. Act as the company's main source of expertise on financial control issues.

## Knowledge, skills and experience required

The job requires:

- a qualified accountant;
- at least 2 years' experience of managing financial control systems and processes;
- experience of managing computerized accounts systems;
- experience of analysing company financial data;
- managerial experience;
- knowledge of the industry;
- good communication skills;
- good IT skills.

## 14. MANAGEMENT ACCOUNTANT

## Main purpose of job

To analyse and report on company financial data to ensure that managers receive timely, accurate and relevant information to enable them to make effective decisions.

## Main responsibilities

1. Consolidate and interpret financial data from various profit and cost centres to ensure that accurate and timely business information is presented to managers to assist them in decision making.
2. Develop and control a centralized accounting system to ensure that accounts are effectively managed.
3. Produce an operating profit and loss account and balance sheet to produce accurate and timely financial information which meets regulatory and business requirements.
4. Monitor expenditure against budgets and advise managers of any significant variances.
5. Prepare year-end accounting and taxation reports to ensure that the company complies with legal and business requirements.
6. Prepare the annual budget for the company and ensure that individual profit and cost centres have all necessary information for effective budget management.
7. Give any necessary advice on management accountancy issues to ensure that managers and staff understand financial and budgetary requirements.
8. Maintain an awareness of developments in the field of management accountancy to ensure the continued provision of a high-quality professional service.

## Knowledge, skills and experience required

The job requires:

- a qualified accountant;
- at least 2 years' experience of management accountancy;
- experience of managing computerized accounts systems;

- experience of analysing company financial data;
- knowledge of the industry;
- good communication skills.

# 15. PAYROLL ASSISTANT

## Main purpose of job

To assist in the payment of staff salaries.

## Main responsibilities

1. Arrange the payment of staff salaries through the computerized payroll system.
2. Administer the Statutory Sick Pay, Statutory Maternity Pay and Statutory Paternity Pay schemes.
3. Assist in the administration of the pension scheme and the personal health insurance scheme.
4. Provide advice to staff and managers on matters related to pay, taxation and National Insurance.
5. Maintain records of expenses incurred by staff and arrange for the payment of these.
6. Maintain all necessary payroll records required to comply with statutory regulations and for the effective management of the payroll.
7. Provide petty cash on request and maintain a record of all payments made.

## Knowledge, skills and experience required

The job requires:

- qualifications to GCSE level including English and Maths;
- previous experience in an accounts office;
- an understanding of payroll procedures;
- accuracy;
- computer and keyboard skills;
- good telephone manner.

# 16. PAYROLL SUPERVISOR

## Main purpose of job

To oversee the accurate and timely payment of staff salaries and expenses, ensuring that appropriate statutory deductions are made.

## Main responsibilities

1. Supervise the accurate and timely payment of all staff salaries and expenses, making the appropriate statutory deductions.
2. Supervise the administration of the permanent health insurance scheme and the pension scheme.
3. Supervise the administration of the Statutory Sick Pay scheme, Statutory Maternity Pay and Statutory Paternity Pay schemes.
4. Provide any required advice and guidance on payroll matters to managers and staff.
5. Oversee the timely and accurate submission of all statutory returns to the Inland Revenue and other government departments.
6. Monitor all payroll costs and ensure that these are allocated to the correct budget heads.
7. Keep abreast of all developments relating to payroll law and administration to ensure that the company complies with its statutory obligations and follows best practice.
8. Develop and implement all necessary systems and procedures to ensure the continued timely and accurate payment of salaries and expenses.
9. Supervise payroll staff to ensure that they are appropriately motivated and trained and carry out their responsibilities effectively.

## Knowledge, skills and experience required

The job requires:

- qualifications to GCSE A level, including English and Maths;
- at least 2 years' payroll experience;
- detailed knowledge of the statutory regulations applying to payroll procedures;
- supervisory skills;

- accuracy;
- computer and keyboard skills;
- good interpersonal skills.

# 17. PRINCIPAL ACCOUNTANT/SECTION HEAD

## Main purpose of job

To direct and control a team of accountancy staff providing full accounting services for a large operating centre.

## Main responsibilities

1. Direct and control accountancy staff to ensure that they are appropriately trained and motivated and carry out their responsibilities to the required standards.
2. Assist in the development of business plans to enable the company to meet its corporate objectives.
3. Provide full accounting services, including the preparation of estimates, annual operating and capital budgets and final accounts for an operating centre.
4. Provide advice and guidance to managers and staff on the interpretation and implementation of financial regulations and accountancy codes of practice.
5. Develop and maintain all other necessary controls and processes to ensure that legal and financial requirements and regulations are complied with.
6. Monitor the financial information system to ensure that timely and accurate information is provided for managerial decision making.
7. Oversee the preparation of statistical returns and financial analysis on a range of topics for internal and external use.
8. Oversee the administration of any loans and repayments, including maintaining liaison with brokers and lenders.
9. Prepare and monitor cash flow projections and associated records to determine the optimum use of funds or the need to raise additional revenue.

## Knowledge, skills and experience required

The job requires:

- an accountancy qualification;

- at least 5 years' post-qualification experience;
- managerial experience;
- good computer skills;
- excellent analytical skills;
- accuracy;
- excellent interpersonal skills.

# 18. SALES LEDGER CLERK

## Main purpose of job

To generate and process invoices and credit notes to ensure effective credit control and cash management.

## Main responsibilities

1. Generate invoices and credit notes in accordance with standard procedures to ensure effective cash and credit control.
2. Prepare sales ledger reconciliations to ensure that transactions are accurately processed and recorded.
3. Prepare and analyse records of invoices and credit notes to assist in financial and management accountancy.
4. Record all transactions to ensure that up-to-date and accurate records are maintained.

## Knowledge, skills and experience required

The job requires:

- good numeracy skills;
- 1 month's general accountancy experience;
- accuracy;
- ability to use computer spreadsheets.

## 19. SENIOR ACCOUNTANT

## Main purpose of job

To supervise a small team of accountancy staff providing full accounting services for a profit centre.

## Main responsibilities

1. Supervise accountancy staff to ensure that they are appropriately trained and motivated and carry out their responsibilities to the required standards.
2. Provide full accounting services, including the preparation of estimates, budgetary control and final accounts for a cost centre.
3. Prepare monthly trading accounts for cost centre activities to ensure that financial targets are met and to assess the need for any remedial action.
4. Develop and maintain all other necessary controls and processes to ensure that legal and financial requirements and regulations are complied with.
5. Monitor the financial information system to ensure that timely and accurate information is provided for managerial decision making.
6. Prepare statistical returns and financial analysis on a range of topics for internal and external use.
7. Oversee the administration of any loans and repayments, including maintaining liaison with brokers and lenders.
8. Prepare and monitor cash flow projections and associated records to determine the optimum use of funds or the need to raise additional revenue.

## Knowledge, skills and experience required

The job requires:

- an accountancy qualification;
- at least 2 years' post-qualification experience;
- supervisory experience;
- good computer skills;

- excellent analytical skills;
- accuracy;
- excellent interpersonal skills.

## 20. SENIOR INTERNAL AUDITOR

## Main purpose of job

To review and evaluate internal control systems and procedures to ensure that management policies are being complied with, assets are safeguarded, information is maintained in a secure and accurate manner and legal requirements are complied with.

## Main responsibilities

1. Review and evaluate internal procedures and supporting documentation to ensure that they provide an effective control system and to identify any weaknesses.
2. Carry out or supervise audits and compliance testing to ensure that procedures are operating effectively with appropriate controls and recommend changes where necessary.
3. Provide information and assistance to managers and staff to enable them to comply with financial and statutory requirements.
4. Carry out reviews of specific functions and processes to promote best value and recommend improvements.
5. Assist in the development of any internal audit programme to ensure that all functions are subject to systematic review.
6. Supervise audit staff to ensure that they carry out their responsibilities effectively.
7. Develop and maintain new systems and procedures to assist managers and staff in complying with financial regulations and meeting their objectives.

## Knowledge, skills and experience required

The job requires:

- qualification at least to Accountancy Technician standard;
- at least 2 years' experience of internal audit;
- general accountancy experience;
- supervisory experience;
- excellent computer skills;

- excellent analytical skills;
- accuracy;
- good interpersonal skills.

# 21. SYSTEMS ACCOUNTANT

## Main purpose of job

To monitor and provide financial reports and information on the company's profit and cost centres to assist managers in making effective financial and operational decisions.

## Main responsibilities

1. Prepare regular and accurate financial reports on the company's profit and cost centres to enable managers to make effective financial and operational decisions.
2. Develop any required systems and procedures to enable the regular and accurate collection of financial and other performance data.
3. Provide advice to managers and staff on data obtained, highlighting any particular problem areas, so that any necessary remedial action can be taken.
4. Assist managers and staff in the development of systems and procedures to enable the effective monitoring and control of financial and performance measures.
5. Assist in the development of any computer systems required for the collection and monitoring of financial and performance data.
6. Carry out various ad hoc projects in relation to financial and performance data.

## Knowledge, skills and experience required

The job requires:

- qualifications to Accountancy Technician standard;
- at least 2 years' experience of financial analysis;
- general accountancy experience;
- excellent computer skills;
- excellent analytical skills;
- accuracy;
- good interpersonal skills.

# 5

# Financial services

This section includes job descriptions for the following jobs:

1. Branch manager (bank)
2. Claims clerk
3. Investment analyst
4. Investment manager
5. Tax manager
6. Underwriter
7. Underwriting and claims manager
8. Underwriting clerk
9. Underwriting manager

# 1. BRANCH MANAGER (BANK)

## Main purpose of job

To direct and control the staff of the branch to meet branch service and sales objectives and to develop and implement a business plan for the branch.

## Main responsibilities

1.  Direct and control the branch team to ensure that they are appropriately motivated and trained and that they achieve their objectives.
2.  Communicate the bank's strategy and policies to staff and ensure that these are effectively implemented.
3.  Control the effective provision of bank services to ensure quality of service and operational integrity in accordance with the bank's strategy and policies.
4.  Monitor and control all branch lending to ensure that it is undertaken in accordance with the bank's credit policy.
5.  Develop and deliver products that meet customer requirements and maximize the return to the branch.
6.  Develop and implement all necessary systems and procedures to ensure the effective delivery of branch services.
7.  Continually reassess the operational risk inherent in the business, taking account of changing economic or market conditions, legal and regulatory requirements, operating procedures and practices, and the impact of new technology.
8.  Promote the bank's image in the community by attendance at internal and external meetings and participation in community activities.

## Knowledge, skills and experience required

The job requires:

*   ACIB or equivalent professional qualification;
*   understanding of the relevant rules under the Financial Services Act and Consumer Credit Act;

- at least 5 years' experience in the banking sector;
- previous experience in a customer services role;
- management skills;
- strong technical knowledge of the bank's products and services;
- strong communication skills;
- commercial awareness;
- business development skills;
- computer literacy.

# 2. CLAIMS CLERK

## Main purpose of job

To review and process claims on behalf of the company and make recommendations for settlement of these.

## Main responsibilities

1. Check claims to assess the nature and extent of any liability.
2. Arrange the appointment of loss adjusters, other estimators and experts for the preparation of estimates to determine the value of claims.
3. Calculate the value of any claims to recommend the amount of any settlement.
4. Negotiate the settlement of claims within limits prescribed by the company with insurers or their representatives.
5. Prepare cheques for settlement of claims and take all necessary action to close the file.
6. Respond to occasional client queries to ensure that these are resolved effectively and sensitively.
7. Maintain all necessary records and prepare data for computer input.

## Knowledge, skills and experience required

The job requires:

- education to GCSE level;
- approximately 1 year's training and experience in claims administration;
- good interpersonal and communication skills;
- good knowledge of company products;
- accuracy.

# 3. INVESTMENT ANALYST

## Main purpose of job

To analyse market trends for securities, bonds and stocks, make recommendations to clients and implement deals in accordance with agreed parameters.

## Main responsibilities

1. Analyse and monitor market trends to be able to make recommendations about investments.
2. Buy and sell stocks, shares etc to produce the maximum possible return.
3. Record all transactions to ensure that dealing costs are correctly calculated.
4. Advise clients or employer on the suitability of investments to ensure the best returns consistent with the investment policy.
5. Research general developments in markets to try to forecast trends.
6. Develop and maintain contacts with brokers and analysts to gain market information.
7. Negotiate deals with brokers and companies on behalf of the client or employer to secure the best possible terms.
8. Maintain an awareness of economic, financial and political developments which might affect market trends.

## Knowledge, skills and experience required

The job requires:

- degree-level education;
- ideally a professional qualification as an actuary or in financial analysis;
- at least 3 years' training and experience in market analysis;
- skills of negotiation, decision making, presentation and use of the telephone;
- analytical skills;
- detailed knowledge of relevant markets.

## 4. INVESTMENT MANAGER

## Main purpose of job

Direct and control the analysis of market trends for securities, bonds and stocks, to be able to determine the company's investment policy.

## Main responsibilities

1. Direct and control a team of analysts to ensure that they are appropriately motivated and trained and carry out their responsibilities to the required standards.
2. Oversee the analysis and monitoring of market trends to be able to make recommendations about investment policy.
3. Determine the rates of return on investments to ensure that investment objectives are achieved and to recommend changes as required.
4. Advise the company on the suitability of investments to ensure the best returns consistent with the investment policy.
5. Research the economic, financial, political and other factors affecting markets and make appropriate recommendations to maximize investment returns to the company.
6. Evaluate investment proposals and recommend those that will produce the best returns consistent with company policy.
7. Develop and implement techniques and processes to analyse risk and likely returns to guide investment selection.
8. Develop and maintain a range of contacts to gain market information.
9. Negotiate deals with brokers and companies on behalf of the company to secure the best possible terms.

## Knowledge, skills and experience required

The job requires:

- degree-level education;
- a professional qualification as an actuary or in financial analysis;
- at least 5 years' training and experience market analysis;
- skills of negotiation, decision making and presentation;

- managerial experience;
- analytical skills;
- organization skills;
- detailed knowledge of relevant markets.

# 5. TAX MANAGER

## Main purpose of job

To develop and implement policies which provide an effective tax planning and management service to the company.

## Main responsibilities

1. Develop and implement all necessary policies and procedures to ensure the effective and optimal planning and management of the company's tax liabilities.
2. Estimate the company's tax liability and advise accountancy staff to ensure that adequate provision is made in company accounts.
3. Oversee the compilation and despatch of all relevant statutory returns, ensuring that these are accurate and meet all deadlines.
4. Discuss and negotiate the company's tax liability with relevant statutory bodies.
5. Analyse the taxation aspects of any agreements made by the company with third parties and advise managers accordingly.
6. Act as the company's principal adviser on all matters relating to taxation to ensure that the company's tax liabilities are optimized.
7. Maintain detailed and up-to-date knowledge of all current tax legislation and other matters which might impact on the company's tax liabilities.

## Knowledge, skills and experience required

The job requires:

- degree-level education;
- a professional qualification in taxation;
- at least 10 years' tax experience;
- skills of negotiation, decision making and presentation;
- analytical skills;
- organization skills;
- detailed knowledge of taxation law and rules.

# 6. UNDERWRITER

## Main purpose of job

To analyse risks and agree insurance premiums up to agreed limits.

## Main responsibilities

1.  Analyse risks by obtaining information from clients and other sources to determine appropriate premium levels.
2.  Respond to enquiries from potential clients, insurance companies and brokers on a range of issues, ensuring that these are dealt with speedily and effectively.
3.  Prepare contract terms for clients and ensure that they are aware of their responsibilities in the contract.
4.  Maintain a sound knowledge of competitors by thoroughly analysing market position, products and rates etc.
5.  Undertake any necessary checks and research on prospective clients to provide the information required for accurate risk assessment.
6.  Promote interest in the company and its products.
7.  Review claims received from clients to check their accuracy and ensure that these are effectively processed.
8.  Monitor clients' performance and circumstances to assess any changes that may be required to premium levels.
9.  Maintain all necessary records and processes to ensure that premiums are paid promptly and that claims are efficiently processed.

## Knowledge, skills and experience required

The job requires:

- at least 2 years' experience in the insurance industry;
- underwriting skills;
- strong technical knowledge of the insurance industry;
- strong negotiating skills;
- commercial awareness;
- computer literacy.

# 7. UNDERWRITING AND CLAIMS MANAGER

## Main purpose of job

To accept risks on behalf of the company which conform to assumptions made in the premium calculations and to ensure that claims made against the company because of death or disability are within the policy terms and payments are made promptly and efficiently to the person authorized.

## Main responsibilities

1. Direct and control the underwriting and claims staff to ensure that they are appropriately motivated and receive all the training and development necessary to carry out their roles effectively.
2. Accept risks that conform to assumptions made in the premium calculations and that are within underwriting policy guidelines.
3. Review underwriting procedures to ensure that application forms produce the information required.
4. Provide guidance and assistance to the sales force, including the preparation of suitable training and publicity material to ensure that they are able to provide a sound service.
5. Contribute to the company's underwriting policy to ensure that mortality and morbidity results are satisfactory.
6. Review claims made against the company because of death or disability to ensure that these are within the policy terms and that all genuine claims are met and paid within 24 hours and non-genuine ones rejected.
7. Respond to occasional client queries to ensure that these are resolved effectively and sensitively.
8. Undertake any necessary research and provide expertise and advice on any matters of general concern and interest to the company in the underwriting and claims fields.

## Knowledge, skills and experience required

The job requires:

- degree-level education;

- approximately 10 years' training and experience in underwriting as well as 5 years' dealing with claims;
- a qualification such as FCII is desirable;
- skills of negotiation, decision making, presentation and use of the telephone;
- a wide knowledge of the life assurance sector;
- managerial experience.

# 8. UNDERWRITING CLERK

## Main purpose of job

To accept more straightforward risks on behalf of the company which conform to established rates and acceptance criteria.

## Main responsibilities

1. Check proposal forms to ensure that risks conform to assumptions made in the premium calculations and are within underwriting policy guidelines.
2. Agree contract terms with proposer in accordance with company guidelines and policy guidelines.
3. Advise proposer of terms and conditions applying to policies.
4. Calculate and agree renewal premiums in accordance with company guidelines.
5. Respond to occasional client queries to ensure that these are resolved effectively and sensitively.
6. Maintain all necessary records and prepare data for computer input.

## Knowledge, skills and experience required

The job requires:

- education to GCSE level;
- approximately 1 year's training and experience in underwriting;
- good interpersonal and communication skills;
- good knowledge of company products;
- accuracy.

# 9. UNDERWRITING MANAGER

## Main purpose of job

To direct and control the underwriting team and to take responsibility for a portfolio of clients, ensuring effective risk management for the company.

## Main responsibilities

1. Direct and control the team to ensure that they are appropriately motivated and trained and that they achieve their objectives.
2. Provide an efficient and effective service to clients by maintaining effective communication with them, responding promptly to enquiries and negotiating contracts.
3. Analyse potential risks and provide reports and recommendations.
4. Maintain a sound knowledge of competitors by thoroughly analysing market position, products, rates etc.
5. Prepare contract terms for clients and ensure that they are aware of their responsibilities in the contract.
6. Review claims from clients, check these for accuracy and decide on the appropriate action to be taken.
7. Maintain all necessary records and processes to ensure that premiums are paid promptly and that claims are efficiently processed.
8. Oversee the underwriting budget to ensure that the company meets its financial targets.

## Knowledge, skills and experience required

The job requires:

- at least 10 years' experience in the insurance industry;
- underwriting skills;
- strong technical knowledge of the insurance sector;
- management skills and previous management experience;
- an ability to undertake analysis and research;
- the excellent interpersonal skills necessary to be able to manage a team of professionals and to negotiate contracts with a range of clients.

# 6

# Human resources/ personnel

This section includes job descriptions for the following jobs:

1. Compensation analyst
2. Compensation and benefits manager
3. Director of organization development
4. Employee relations manager
5. Employee relations officer
6. Health and safety manager
7. Human resource planning manager
8. Job analyst
9. Job evaluator
10. Personnel assistant (recruitment)
11. Personnel assistant (training)
12. Personnel director
13. Personnel manager
14. Personnel officer
15. Recruitment consultant
16. Recruitment manager

17. Recruitment officer
18. Senior personnel officer
19. Training and development manager

# 1. COMPENSATION ANALYST

## Main purpose of job

To provide administrative support and carry out research in relation to the organization's compensation and benefits policies.

## Main responsibilities

1. Maintain administrative procedures in support of the organization's compensation and benefits policies to ensure that these are implemented effectively.
2. Maintain staff information systems to ensure that the organization has accurate and up-to-date pay and benefits data relating to all staff.
3. Carry out and participate in salary surveys, and analyse data, to ensure that the organization has accurate and up-to-date information relating to external pay relativities.
4. Advise managers and staff on reward issues.
5. Carry out research on reward issues to ensure that the organization is applying policies that are in line with market practice.
6. Evaluate jobs using a standard job evaluation scheme and provide administrative support to job evaluation panels.

## Knowledge, skills and experience required

The job requires:

- qualification to degree level;
- studying for membership of the Chartered Institute of Personnel and Development;
- at least 2 years' experience in a related role;
- high-level skills in numerical and statistical analysis;
- computer skills;
- good human relations skills.

## 2. COMPENSATION AND BENEFITS MANAGER

## Main purpose of job

To develop and implement policies and procedures to ensure that the organization's compensation and benefits are sufficient to attract and retain the required number of staff of the right calibre.

## Main responsibilities

1. Develop and implement reward policies and procedures which ensure that the organization is able to attract and retain the required number of staff with the appropriate skills and experience to be able to achieve its business objectives.
2. Advise managers and staff on all reward issues.
3. Assist in negotiations with staff and unions on all reward and related issues to ensure that the full implications of reward policies are taken into account.
4. Develop and coordinate the implementation of incentive schemes for managers and staff to ensure that these achieve their objectives.
5. Carry out or commission research on reward issues to ensure that the organization is applying policies that are in line with market practice.
6. Regularly review reward policies and practices to ensure that they are in line with market practice and meet their objectives.
7. Monitor all systems and processes for maintaining internal relativities, such as a job evaluation scheme, to ensure these are operating effectively.
8. Negotiate contracts with external consultants and commission reviews to provide the organization with information on market practice in relation to rewards.
9. Maintain comprehensive salary and reward data to ensure that decisions are made in the light of the best possible information.
10. Keep up to date with developments in the field of reward to ensure that the organization continues to apply the best reward practices.

## Knowledge, skills and experience required

The job requires:

- qualification to degree level;
- membership of the Chartered Institute of Personnel and Development;
- at least 5 years' experience in a related role;
- good knowledge of the organization;
- high-level skills in numerical and statistical analysis;
- computer skills;
- excellent human relations skills.

## 3. DIRECTOR OF ORGANIZATION DEVELOPMENT

### Main purpose of job

To develop and implement strategies to improve operations and service delivery and to provide advice and guidance on all aspects of organization development and change.

### Main responsibilities

1.  Direct and control the staff of the department to ensure that they are appropriately motivated and trained and carry out their responsibilities to the required standards.
2.  Contribute to the development of strategies that will help to achieve the organization's mission and core objectives.
3.  Provide advice and guidance to managers and staff on all aspects of organization development and change.
4.  Develop and implement an action plan for managing and achieving changes that will support the organization's core objectives.
5.  Develop and monitor budgets for all major organization development projects.
6.  Negotiate contracts with external consultants and other organizations to provide services in support of organization change and development where these cannot be met from in-house resources.
7.  Develop close working relationships with other key functions in the organization to ensure that there is a coordinated approach to organization change.
8.  Maintain an awareness of developments in the fields of organization change and development to ensure that the organization continues to take advantage of the latest thinking in these areas.
9.  Commission research in the field of organization development and change to ensure that the organization implements policies and approaches that will improve operational effectiveness.

### Knowledge, skills and experience required

The job requires:

*   education to degree level;

- professional qualifications in a relevant discipline;
- considerable experience of managing organization change;
- at least 5 years' senior management experience;
- excellent interpersonal skills;
- excellent analytical skills;
- excellent written and verbal communication skills.

## 4. EMPLOYEE RELATIONS MANAGER

## Main purpose of job

To develop and implement policies and procedures to provide an effective employee relations service and to encourage harmonious industrial relations in the organization.

## Main responsibilities

1. Develop and implement all necessary policies and procedures to promote effective communication between management and staff and to encourage harmonious industrial relations.
2. Supervise employee relations staff to ensure that they are appropriately motivated and trained and carry out their responsibilities to the required standards.
3. Plan and organize the effective communication of all personnel policies to employees.
4. Negotiate joint agreements with employee representatives and shop stewards.
5. Devise and maintain all joint consultative committee machinery to ensure an effective two-way communication process between management and employees.
6. Agree the appointment of shop stewards, safety representatives and/or employee representatives and ensure that appropriate facilities are made available to them.
7. Carry out all necessary research to provide information to support negotiations on pay and conditions.
8. Advise managers on all aspects of employee relations and on the interpretation of joint agreements.
9. Support managers at disciplinary or grievance hearings, or in the event of collective disputes or industrial action.
10. Maintain up-to-date knowledge about employment law as it relates to employee relations.

# Knowledge, skills and experience required

The job requires:

- qualification to degree level;
- membership of the Chartered Institute of Personnel and Development;
- at least 10 years' experience in a related role;
- good knowledge of employment law;
- thorough knowledge of all employment terms and conditions;
- good knowledge of the organization;
- high-level negotiation skills;
- excellent written communication skills;
- research and analytical skills;
- excellent human relations skills.

## 5. EMPLOYEE RELATIONS OFFICER

## Main purpose of job

To implement policies and procedures to provide an effective employee relations service and to encourage harmonious industrial relations in the organization.

## Main responsibilities

1. Apply all necessary policies and procedures to promote effective communication between management and staff and to encourage harmonious industrial relations.
2. Assist in communicating all personnel policies to employees.
3. Consult employee representatives and shop stewards about joint agreements, terms and conditions of employment and other work-related issues.
4. Attend and keep minutes of joint consultative committee meetings and ensure that any required follow-up action is taken.
5. Carry out research to provide information to support negotiations on pay and conditions.
6. Advise managers on all aspects of employee relations and on the interpretation of joint agreements.
7. Support managers at disciplinary or grievance hearings, or in the event of collective disputes or industrial action.
8. Maintain up-to-date knowledge about employment law as it relates to employee relations.

## Knowledge, skills and experience required

The job requires:

- qualification to degree level;
- membership of the Chartered Institute of Personnel and Development;
- at least 5 years' experience in a related role;
- good knowledge of employment law;
- good knowledge of the organization;
- thorough knowledge of all employment terms and conditions;

- high-level negotiation skills;
- excellent written communication skills;
- research and analytical skills;
- excellent human relations skills.

## 6. HEALTH AND SAFETY MANAGER

## Main purpose of job

To develop any necessary policies and procedures to ensure the health and safety of all employees, contractors and visitors to the company and to provide the main source of expert advice on health and safety matters to the company.

## Main responsibilities

1.  Develop policies and procedures to ensure the health and safety of all employees, contractors and visitors to the company.
2.  Provide the main source of advice and guidance to the company and its managers on health and safety matters.
3.  Monitor the company's operations, processes and procedures to ensure that they comply with health and safety regulations.
4.  Investigate and report on accidents and related incidents, recommending any changes that may be necessary, to ensure that the company complies with health and safety regulations.
5.  Carry out a risk analysis for the company and recommend any changes that may be necessary.
6.  Maintain good working relationships with insurers and other relevant authorities to ensure that the company's interests are safeguarded and a safe and healthy working environment is maintained.
7.  Provide any necessary training to managers and staff to ensure that they comply with all health and safety requirements.
8.  Set up and maintain health and safety consultative machinery and provide all required training and facilities for safety representatives to ensure that the company meets its statutory requirements.
9.  Monitor facilities and internal procedures for recruitment, training and retention to ensure that the company meets its requirements under the provisions of the Disability Discrimination Act.
10. Review working practices and safety equipment to ensure that the company meets the requirements of insurers and other relevant bodies.

11.   Maintain an awareness of developments in the field of health and safety to ensure that the company continues to comply with best practice and legal requirements.

## Knowledge, skills and experience required

The job requires:

- a relevant health and safety qualification;
- at least 5 years' experience of health and safety in a similar environment;
- experience in a similar industry;
- good communication skills.

## 7. HUMAN RESOURCE PLANNING MANAGER

## Main purpose of job

To develop and implement policies and procedures to ensure that the existing and future staffing needs of the organization are met.

## Main responsibilities

1. Develop and implement policies and procedures to ensure that the organization's staffing needs are met.
2. Analyse business plans to determine likely future staffing needs.
3. Maintain comprehensive organization charts and staffing lists to identify current staffing and vacancy data.
4. Develop planning models to enable future staffing needs to be determined accurately.
5. Advise the organization on the staffing implications of new policies, products and services.
6. Develop and maintain information systems to ensure the accurate collection and maintenance of staffing data.
7. Develop procedures to ensure that all data is maintained in an accurate, up-to-date and confidential manner, supports the organization's policies on diversity and equal opportunities and complies with the Data Protection Act.

## Knowledge, skills and experience required

The job requires:

- qualification to degree level;
- membership of the Chartered Institute of Personnel and Development;
- at least 3 years' experience in a related role;
- good knowledge of the organization;
- high-level skills in numerical and statistical analysis;
- computer skills;
- good human relations skills.

# 8. JOB ANALYST

## Main purpose of job

To interview jobholders and write job descriptions for job evaluation and other purposes.

## Main responsibilities

1. Interview jobholders, supervisors and managers to get information about jobs as a basis for preparing job descriptions.
2. Draft job descriptions for review and approval by jobholders and their line managers.
3. Prepare and implement an interview schedule to ensure that job descriptions are completed by agreed deadlines.
4. Maintain contact with jobholders, line managers and personnel staff to ensure that information in job descriptions is accurate and up to date.
5. Where necessary, observe jobs being carried out to enable job descriptions to be prepared.

## Knowledge, skills and experience required

The job requires:

- education to degree level;
- at least 1 year's experience in the personnel function;
- an understanding of the job evaluation process;
- excellent interviewing and interpersonal skills;
- analytical skills;
- an ability to write concisely and clearly.

## 9. JOB EVALUATOR

## Main purpose of job

To evaluate jobs from prepared job descriptions so that they can be allocated to the appropriate grades or pay rates.

## Main responsibilities

1. Evaluate jobs from prepared job descriptions and allocate a points score, using an agreed job evaluation method.
2. Record evaluation results and the reasons for these.
3. Organize and attend job evaluation panels to evaluate groups of jobs.
4. Review job evaluation results to ensure that these are logical in relation to the whole organization.
5. Train staff in the job evaluation process.
6. Design and implement job evaluation methods and processes which provide an objective, accurate and consistent means of measuring job size.
7. Advise managers and staff of the organization on job evaluation and equal value issues.
8. Design pay and grading structures arising from the job evaluation process.
9. Carry out salary surveys to determine external relativities.
10. Design and communicate all necessary job evaluation manuals, forms, records and other procedures to ensure that the organization maintains accurate and up-to-date job evaluation data.
11. Keep up to date with developments in the fields of job evaluation, equal value and related employment law to ensure that the organization continues to have accurate advice.
12. Where necessary, carry out job analysis to prepare accurate job descriptions.

## Knowledge, skills and experience required

The job requires:

- education to degree level;

- membership of the Chartered Institute of Personnel and Development;
- at least 3 years' experience in job evaluation and job analysis;
- thorough understanding of job evaluation schemes in use;
- thorough knowledge of the company's pay structure;
- excellent communication and interpersonal skills;
- excellent analytical skills;
- an ability to write concisely and clearly.

## 10. PERSONNEL ASSISTANT (RECRUITMENT)

## Main purpose of job

To support the personnel manager in the provision of a high quality and professional personnel service by providing administrative support on recruitment procedures.

## Main responsibilities

1. Place job advertisements, where necessary in association with recruitment agencies, and send out application forms and job information packs to potential job applicants.
2. Arrange interviews and make any necessary arrangements for pre-employment checks and tests.
3. Deal with all routine correspondence to applicants, including writing to successful and unsuccessful job applicants.
4. Send out offer letters and statements of terms and conditions of employment to successful applicants.
5. Coordinate arrangements for introducing new staff into the company, including staff induction.
6. Assist in dealing with routine questions relating to terms and conditions of employment from existing staff, managers and applicants.
7. Set up and maintain a personal file for every new employee and ensure that these are maintained in an accurate and up-to-date manner.
8. Maintain the personnel database and prepare reports as required to provide information to management.
9. Maintain the staff handbook in an accurate and up-to-date condition.
10. Make any necessary arrangements for the recruitment of temporary staff as requested by managers.

## Knowledge, skills and experience required

The job requires:

- education to GCSE A level;

- studying for CIPD qualification;
- experience of office systems;
- good communication skills;
- accuracy;
- good interpersonal skills;
- ability to organize own workload;
- tact and discretion.

## 11. PERSONNEL ASSISTANT (TRAINING)

### Main purpose of job

To support the personnel manager in the provision of a high quality and professional personnel service by providing administrative support on training services.

### Main responsibilities

1.  Maintain up-to-date and accurate training records for all staff.
2.  Maintain an up-to-date and accurate database of training suppliers and course programmes.
3.  Arrange staff attendance on in-house and external training programmes, including payment of all invoices and expenses.
4.  Make all necessary administrative arrangements for the running of in-house training courses.

### Knowledge, skills and experience required

The job requires:

- education to GCSE A level;
- studying for CIPD qualification;
- experience of office systems;
- good communication skills;
- accuracy;
- good interpersonal skills;
- ability to organize own workload;
- tact and discretion.

## 12. PERSONNEL DIRECTOR

## Main purpose of job

To help ensure that the company achieves its corporate objectives and makes the best use of its employees by developing and maintaining innovative, effective and forward-looking human resource strategies, practices and procedures.

## Main responsibilities

1.  Contribute to the development of the company's corporate strategy, particularly by advising on the human resource implications of strategic decisions.
2.  Develop and maintain appropriate and effective personnel strategies and ensure that these are communicated and implemented throughout the company in a way that supports corporate objectives.
3.  Develop and maintain all necessary personnel planning, recruitment and selection procedures to ensure that the company has staff of the right calibre to enable it to meet its corporate objectives.
4.  Develop and maintain a remuneration strategy and appropriate terms and conditions of employment to ensure that the company is able to attract, retain and motivate staff.
5.  Advise the senior managers of the company about the personnel policies, procedures and actions required to ensure that the company makes the best use of its employees.
6.  Develop and maintain all necessary training policies and procedures to ensure that all staff are trained and developed to the standards required.
7.  Maintain an awareness of the requirements of employment legislation to ensure that the company complies with all legal requirements and to provide sound advice to management.
8.  Encourage and maintain sound employee relations by undertaking all necessary consultation and negotiation with employee representatives and by ensuring the effective communication of company policies.

9.  Develop and maintain all necessary personnel procedures and information systems to ensure that the company has all the information required for effective resource planning and management and regulatory compliance.
10. Direct and control the staff of the personnel department to ensure that they undertake their responsibilities effectively and within budget.
11. Develop and monitor the personnel budget to ensure that personnel services are provided at the appropriate level consistent with the attainment of the company's corporate objectives.

## Knowledge, skills and experience required

The job requires:

- education to degree level;
- at least 10 years' generalist personnel experience;
- membership of the Chartered Institute of Personnel and Development (MCIPD);
- extensive management experience;
- knowledge of the industry;
- an ability to develop strategy;
- leadership skills;
- excellent interpersonal skills;
- excellent negotiating skills;
- an eye for detail;
- analytical ability;
- good organizing skills.

# 13. PERSONNEL MANAGER

## Main purpose of job

To direct and control the personnel department to provide a comprehensive and professional personnel support service to the company.

## Main responsibilities

1.  Direct and control the staff of the department to ensure that they are appropriately motivated and trained and carry out their responsibilities to the required standards.
2.  Develop and implement personnel policies to support business goals and to ensure that the company complies with legal requirements and best practice.
3.  Define the quality standards to be applied in the management of the company's staff and monitor these to ensure that a high quality personnel service continues to be provided to the company.
4.  Develop, implement and monitor all required personnel procedures relating to staff terms and conditions of employment to ensure that the company complies with legal requirements and best practice.
5.  Provide a comprehensive personnel advisory service to all company managers and staff to ensure that the company follows best practice in the management of its staff and to ensure compliance with legal requirements.
6.  Research and develop personnel policies which will ensure that the company recruits and retains a pool of well-trained and highly motivated staff.
7.  Provide an employee relations service to the company, including negotiating with employee representatives on personnel issues, to ensure that harmonious relationships and effective communications are maintained between management and staff.
8.  Identify the company's staffing needs and develop policies and procedures to ensure that the required numbers and types of staff are recruited within agreed budgets to meet operational requirements.

9.  Recommend and implement reward policies and structures which ensure the effective recruitment and retention of high quality employees.
10. Maintain comprehensive personnel records to ensure compliance with Equal Opportunities and other legal requirements and to provide information on staffing issues to the company and other relevant bodies.

## Knowledge, skills and experience required

The job requires:

- a degree;
- at least 5 years' generalist personnel experience;
- membership of the Chartered Institute of Personnel and Development (MCIPD);
- management experience;
- knowledge of the industry;
- excellent interpersonal skills;
- excellent negotiating skills;
- an eye for detail;
- analytical ability;
- good organizing skills.

# 14. PERSONNEL OFFICER

## Main purpose of job

To support the personnel manager in the provision of a high quality and professional personnel service through the effective administration of the personnel department's systems and procedures and by providing a recruitment and advisory service to managers and employees.

## Main responsibilities

1. Assist in the administration of all personnel policies and procedures.
2. Provide advice to line managers on best practice in all aspects of employment, including company policies and legislation.
3. Provide an advisory service to all employees and employee representatives on company employment policies and procedures.
4. Maintain regular contact with managers to establish their recruitment needs and carry out all necessary procedures to meet those needs.
5. Monitor and record absence levels in each department and provide statistical data to managers in relation to these.
6. Monitor and apply personnel policies and procedures as directed by the personnel manager.
7. Analyse job requirements and prepare job descriptions and person specifications for recruitment, job evaluation and other purposes.

## Knowledge, skills and experience required

The job requires:

- education to GCSE A level;
- studying for full membership of CIPD;
- a minimum of 6 months' personnel experience;
- good organizational skills;
- good communication skills.

## 15. RECRUITMENT CONSULTANT

## Main purpose of job

To market and sell recruitment assignments in a specific industry sector or geographical area to meet business targets in accordance with the company's quality standards.

## Main responsibilities

1. Market and sell recruitment assignments to clients in a specific industry sector or geographical area to ensure that all sales and revenue targets are met.
2. Undertake the various stages of the recruitment process, as required by the client, to the company's quality standards.
3. Maintain and review a register of candidates appropriate to any potential client requirements and undertake interviews of candidates to determine their suitability where necessary.
4. Maintain all necessary client and candidate records and appropriate supporting systems to ensure that there is accurate and up-to-date information in accordance with relevant quality standards and statutory requirements.
5. Carry out all required pre-employment checks to ensure that candidates are appropriately qualified for jobs being filled.
6. Undertake any necessary market research to ensure that the service provided is up to date and appropriate to clients' needs.

## Knowledge, skills and experience required

The job requires:

- qualification to degree level;
- ideally a relevant professional qualification;
- a minimum of 1 year's recruitment consultancy experience;
- thorough knowledge of the industry sector in which the job operates;
- an ability to market and sell services;
- excellent interpersonal and negotiating skills;
- good organizational skills.

## 16. RECRUITMENT MANAGER

## Main purpose of job

To oversee the recruitment and selection process to ensure that the organization attracts and recruits suitable applicants for identified vacancies.

## Main responsibilities

1. Supervise section staff to ensure that they are appropriately motivated and trained and carry out their responsibilities to the required standards.
2. Develop and oversee the implementation of the organization's recruitment strategy to ensure that staffing needs are met.
3. Develop and oversee the implementation of all necessary systems and procedures to ensure that the recruitment and selection process operates effectively.
4. Supervise the process for the placing of advertisements for all internal and external vacancies.
5. Negotiate contracts with external advertising and recruitment consultants to secure the most favourable terms for the organization.
6. Interview potential recruits and appoint staff in consultation with the appropriate line managers.
7. Oversee all administrative arrangements relating to the recruitment and selection process, including arranging tests and providing suitable arrangements for applicants with special needs.
8. Keep up to date with the latest developments in the field of recruitment and selection.

## Knowledge, skills and experience required

The job requires:

- qualification to degree level;
- studying for membership of the Chartered Institute of Personnel and Development;
- at least 3 years' experience in a related role;

- good knowledge of the organization;
- supervisory skills;
- administrative skills and experience;
- good human relations skills.

# 17. RECRUITMENT OFFICER

## Main purpose of job

To attract and recruit applicants to a range of jobs in the organization and to carry out all associated administration.

## Main responsibilities

1. Maintain up-to-date and accurate lists of jobs and vacancies within the organization to be able to identify staffing needs.
2. Advertise all vacancies internally through in-house magazines, the intranet and notice boards.
3. Draft copy for external advertisements, decide appropriate media for external advertisements and negotiate advertising space with selected media.
4. Identify and maintain regular contact with external advertising and recruitment agencies to support the recruitment process.
5. Design and send out any required application forms and supporting documentation in relation to advertised vacancies.
6. Sift applications received to identify the most suitable applicants for jobs.
7. Interview potential recruits to identify those suitable for shortlisting.
8. Carry out all administrative arrangements for those attending a selection process, including arranging tests and providing suitable arrangements for applicants with special needs.
9. Obtain references and carry out required pre-employment checks to ensure that information given is verified and candidates have the right to work in the UK.
10. Prepare all documentation relating to appointments including offer and rejection letters.

## Knowledge, skills and experience required

The job requires:

- qualification to degree level;

- studying for membership of the Chartered Institute of Personnel and Development;
- at least 2 years' experience in a related role;
- good knowledge of the organization;
- administrative skills and experience;
- good human relations skills.

# 18. SENIOR PERSONNEL OFFICER

## Main purpose of job

To support the personnel manager in the provision of a high quality and professional personnel service by providing advice and guidance on a range of personnel issues and by developing the appropriate policies and procedures to ensure that employment law and best practice are adhered to.

## Main responsibilities

1. Assist in the development of personnel policies and procedures to ensure that the company follows best practice and avoids infringing employment law.
2. Assist in organizational change projects to improve the overall efficiency and effectiveness of the company.
3. Monitor, evaluate and participate in the company's recruitment and selection process to ensure that the company recruits the best people for available jobs and complies with legislation and best practice relating to equal opportunities and discrimination.
4. Maintain all necessary personnel records to effectively monitor sickness levels, implementation of equal opportunities policies, staffing levels etc.
5. Provide advice to managers on a range of employment issues to ensure that they manage their staff in accordance with best practice and legal requirements.
6. Prepare letters, policies and other documents in relation to terms and conditions of employment to ensure that the company complies with legal requirements.
7. Maintain a reference library of employment law information to ensure that the company continues to be up to date and in compliance with the most recent employment legislation.
8. Provide support and advice to managers on the planning of their workforce requirements.
9. Analyse job requirements and prepare job descriptions and person specifications for recruitment, job evaluation and other purposes.

## Knowledge, skills and experience required

The job requires:

- membership of the CIPD;
- at least 5 years' experience in the HR field;
- knowledge of the company and the industry;
- excellent interpersonal skills;
- tact and discretion;
- analytical skills.

# 19. TRAINING AND DEVELOPMENT MANAGER

## Main purpose of job

To provide a comprehensive training and development service to the company to ensure that all staff achieve high professional standards and that they have the necessary skills to help the company attain its strategic objectives.

## Main responsibilities

1.  Develop a training and development strategy for the company to support the company's business plan and to ensure that staff have the necessary skills to meet their objectives and the opportunity to develop to the maximum of their potential.
2.  Direct and control the staff of the department to ensure that they are appropriately motivated and trained to be able to carry out their responsibilities to the required standards.
3.  Undertake regular assessments of training needs and develop a programme to meet identified needs.
4.  Maintain close communication with managers and staff to discuss training needs and to ensure that they are fully aware of training opportunities available.
5.  Keep managers and staff informed of internal and external training and development opportunities.
6.  Arrange internal training and development programmes, using external suppliers and consultants as required to meet identified training needs.
7.  Develop and monitor the company's training budget to ensure that the best quality of training and development is provided within the established budget.
8.  Oversee the development of effective processes for the evaluation of all training and development provided.
9.  Maintain an awareness of developments in the training and development field to ensure that the company continues to take advantage of best practice.
10. Oversee the maintenance of all necessary training and development records.

## Knowledge, skills and experience required

The job requires:

- a degree-level qualification;
- membership of the Chartered Institute of Personnel and Development (MCIPD);
- at least 5 years' experience in training and development;
- sound knowledge of the industry;
- a sound understanding of the principles of training and development;
- excellent interpersonal skills;
- excellent communication skills;
- managerial experience;
- excellent planning and organizing skills.

# 7

# Information technology

This section includes job descriptions for the following jobs:

1. Analyst programmer
2. Computer operator
3. Data entry clerk
4. Data preparation supervisor
5. Database manager
6. Director of information technology
7. IT manager
8. IT project coordinator
9. Information systems manager
10. PC support officer
11. Programmer
12. Software design manager
13. Systems analyst
14. Web site designer

# 1. ANALYST PROGRAMMER

## Main purpose of job

To assess the company's information technology requirements and deliver appropriate hardware and software solutions related to those requirements.

## Main responsibilities

1. Determine information system requirements through a detailed analysis of existing systems and procedures and by interviewing key personnel.
2. Define system requirements and recommend appropriate hardware and software solutions.
3. Plan and carry out the testing of recommended information technology solutions to ensure that these perform to the users' requirements.
4. Identify and design all necessary procedures and documentation to support recommended modifications.
5. Present recommended solutions to managers and staff to ensure that they are aware of and support these changes.
6. Develop and maintain contacts with software suppliers to ensure that any proposed modifications are produced in accordance with specification.
7. Train managers and staff in any new or modified systems and procedures.
8. Support managers and staff in the identification and resolution of any day-to-day operating problems arising from the application of new or modified systems and procedures.
9. Maintain an awareness of developments in the computing field to ensure that the company continues to apply the technology most appropriate to its needs.

## Knowledge, skills and experience required

The job requires:

- a degree or equivalent in a relevant field;

- at least 2 years' experience of systems analysis and programming;
- a thorough knowledge of programming languages and supporting software;
- programming skills;
- good analytical skills;
- good communication and presentation skills.

# 2. COMPUTER OPERATOR

## Main purpose of job

To operate a mainframe computer, including data input and retrieval, to meet scheduled output requirements.

## Main responsibilities

1. Carry out all initial actions to ensure that the computer is correctly started up.
2. Load computer with any required consumables.
3. Check that all systems and peripherals are working properly and take remedial action where necessary.
4. Enter data into the computer through a console and keyboard.
5. Retrieve data from the computer and produce reports as required.
6. Monitor systems operation and carry out periodic checks to ensure continued effective running.

## Knowledge, skills and experience required

The job requires:

- detailed knowledge of the computer's operating processes;
- awareness of the work schedules.

## 3. DATA ENTRY CLERK

## Main purpose of job

To enter data into a computer and retrieve data as requested.

## Main responsibilities

1. Receive and check data for computer input.
2. Enter data into the computer through a console and keyboard.
3. Retrieve data from the computer and produce reports as required.

## Knowledge, skills and experience required

The job requires:

- keyboard skills;
- accuracy;
- awareness of work schedules.

## 4. DATA PREPARATION SUPERVISOR

## Main purpose of job

To supervise the computerized data entry and retrieval process.

## Main responsibilities

1. Supervise data entry staff to ensure that they are appropriately trained and carry out their tasks to the required standard.
2. Receive documents for data entry, schedule work and allocate to data entry clerks.
3. Assist in the recruitment and testing of new staff.
4. Resolve any problems relating to data entry or the allocation of staff to meet output requirements.
5. Maintain all required records relating to output, staff attendance and holidays etc.
6. Carry out routine data processing tasks as necessary.

## Knowledge, skills and experience required

The job requires:

- thorough knowledge of all aspects of data entry;
- knowledge of the wider requirements of the business;
- supervisory skills;
- keyboard skills;
- accuracy;
- awareness of work schedules.

# 5. DATABASE MANAGER

## Main purpose of job

To organize and control the organization's database to ensure the efficient management of information to support management decision making and to meet statutory requirements.

## Main responsibilities

1. Direct and control the database management team to ensure that they are appropriately motivated and trained and carry out their responsibilities to the required standard.
2. Organize and control the central database and all data input and output to ensure that information required for management decision making and statutory compliance is accurate and provided at the right time.
3. Develop and implement systems and processes to ensure the accurate and timely collection, analysis and publication of data and information.
4. Publish regular performance reports and ad hoc reports as required to enable managers to monitor progress against organization objectives.
5. Regularly monitor data systems and processes to ensure that information provided continues to be accurate, produced at the right time and maintained in accordance with data protection legislation.
6. Provide an organization-wide advisory and consultancy service on all aspects of data management.
7. Maintain an awareness of developments in the storage and handling of data and review the application of new technologies to improve administrative processes.

## Knowledge, skills and experience required

The job requires:

- a degree in a relevant subject;
- thorough knowledge of all aspects of data entry;

- at least 5 years' data management experience;
- knowledge of the wider requirements of the business;
- managerial experience;
- excellent analytical skills;
- excellent interpersonal skills.

# 6. DIRECTOR OF INFORMATION TECHNOLOGY

## Main purpose of job

To direct and control the development, implementation and maintenance of the company's information and communications strategy and systems to support the business objectives of the company.

## Main responsibilities

1. Direct and control the staff of the information technology and communications department to ensure that they are well motivated and receive all necessary training and development to enable them to carry out their responsibilities to the required standards.

2. Contribute to the development of the company's strategic and business plans, particularly in relation to information technology and communications systems, in support of the company's mission and core objectives.

3. Develop an annual business plan and operating budget for the department and monitor the implementation of these to ensure that financial targets are met.

4. Negotiate service level agreements with internal customers and service providers and monitor service delivery to ensure that agreed targets and standards are met.

5. Negotiate contracts with external providers for services and products which cannot be provided internally and monitor service delivery to ensure that agreed targets and standards are met.

6. Oversee the development and implementation of company-wide information and communications systems which provide all required support to company operations.

7. Oversee the management of all data and information flows within the company to ensure that comprehensive and accurate management information is available as required.

8. Provide a company-wide source of expertise on information technology and communications to ensure that managers and staff have the best possible information for effective decision making and accessing data.

9.  Develop and implement a comprehensive and effective help desk service to provide technical support to systems users.

## Knowledge, skills and experience required

The job requires:

- a degree in a computer-related subject;
- membership of relevant professional body;
- at least 5 years' experience in the design, development and implementation of information technology and communications systems;
- comprehensive experience of developing management information and communications systems;
- substantial management experience and experience of managing budgets;
- a broad understanding of computer systems, computer applications and operating systems;
- analytical and problem-solving skills;
- excellent interpersonal skills;
- negotiation skills.

# 7. IT MANAGER

## Main purpose of job

To direct and control the development, implementation and maintenance of the company's information technology systems to support the business objectives of the company.

## Main responsibilities

1. Develop and implement an information technology strategy to support the financial and business objectives of the company.
2. Develop appropriate computerized information systems to meet the needs of managers and staff.
3. Direct and control the staff of the department to ensure that they are appropriately motivated and trained and that they carry out their responsibilities to the required standard.
4. Establish and maintain all necessary information technology procedures and ensure that all systems are supported by the necessary documentation and manuals.
5. Help to define IT training needs and provide training as required to ensure the most effective use of computer systems.
6. Identify areas in which the introduction of new technology will improve business performance and assist managers with the implementation of any new systems.
7. Develop a programme of maintenance and support for all IT systems to ensure a minimum of downtime and fast resolution of any problems.
8. Provide a source of advice to managers and staff on information technology issues.
9. Maintain an awareness of new developments in information technology and ensure that the company makes the best use of any such developments.

## Knowledge, skills and experience required

The job requires:

● a degree in a computer-related subject;

- at least 5 years' experience in the design, development and implementation of information technology systems;
- a broad understanding of computer systems, computer applications and operating systems;
- analytical and problem-solving skills;
- good communication skills;
- managerial experience.

# 8. IT PROJECT COORDINATOR

## Main purpose of job

To plan and coordinate major IT projects within the organization to ensure that effective IT solutions are delivered within agreed time-scales and costs.

## Main responsibilities

1. Assist in the development of IT project plans across the organization to ensure that effective systems are introduced to meet identified needs.
2. Monitor the implementation of IT projects to ensure that all targets are reached and that the overall project is completed in accordance with agreed timescales and costs.
3. Identify user requirements and develop project and product specifications that will ensure that these requirements are met.
4. Develop and implement any necessary procedures and documentation required to support new IT systems and procedures.
5. Provide suitable training in new systems to users and managers to ensure that they make the optimum use of these systems.
6. Conduct post project evaluations to ensure that systems implemented are operating effectively and providing the services required by users.
7. Represent the department on project teams to ensure that the best possible advice is given about the implications of any new IT systems and proposed changes.
8. Maintain an awareness of developments in the IT field and act as a source of advice and expertise to managers and staff within the company.

## Knowledge, skills and experience required

The job requires:

- qualification to at least HNC level in a computing related field;
- at least 3 years' experience in developing and implementing major IT projects;

- wide knowledge of IT systems and of the latest developments in these;
- good knowledge of the organization;
- excellent analytical skills;
- good interpersonal skills;
- systems analysis skills.

## 9. INFORMATION SYSTEMS MANAGER

## Main purpose of job

To ensure that the company meets its performance targets through the development and maintenance of information systems.

## Main responsibilities

1.  Develop and maintain the company's information systems to ensure that they support the attainment of business objectives.
2.  Develop and maintain the information systems budget to ensure that expenditure is accurately forecasted and kept within agreed limits.
3.  Introduce all necessary security measures to ensure that data systems are secure from data loss or misuse.
4.  Monitor all key management systems to ensure that any problems are rapidly dealt with and any defects remedied.
5.  Provide any required management information to assist with effective decision making.
6.  Develop systems as necessary to meet changing business needs.
7.  Provide training and advice as required to users of information systems to ensure that they make the best use of those systems.
8.  Manage systems projects to ensure that results are delivered within agreed timescales and budgets.
9.  Maintain an awareness of developments in the information systems field to ensure that the company continues to follow best practice.
10.  Direct and control information systems staff to ensure that they are appropriately motivated and trained and carry out their responsibilities to the required standard.

## Knowledge, skills and experience required

The job requires:

- a relevant technical qualification;
- at least 5 years' experience of operating computer systems;
- knowledge of computer-based accounting and business packages;

- a broad range of technical computer skills;
- knowledge of the industry;
- good communication skills;
- managerial skills.

# 10. PC SUPPORT OFFICER

## Main purpose of job

To provide technical support to company staff to help them resolve any software and hardware problems with computers and other technology.

## Main responsibilities

1. Respond to enquiries from staff to help them resolve any hardware or software problems.
2. Maintain a log of any software or hardware problems detected.
3. Support users in the use of computer equipment by providing any necessary training and advice.
4. Maintain a list of suppliers and other subcontractors who may be required to assist in the resolution of technical problems.
5. Arrange for external technical support where problems cannot be resolved in-house.
6. Recommend suitable software and hardware systems where these might improve performance.

## Knowledge, skills and experience required

The job requires:

- technical training in the software and hardware systems used;
- at least 1 year's experience in resolving computer software and hardware problems;
- wide knowledge of office software applications;
- good knowledge of PCs and fault finding;
- good analytical skills;
- good interpersonal skills.

## 11. PROGRAMMER

## Main purpose of job

To design and implement computer programs, and modify existing programs, to meet identified user requirements and to improve the efficiency and effectiveness of the company.

## Main responsibilities

1. Analyse user requirements and identify programming solutions using a range of tools such as flow diagrams, decision trees etc.
2. Develop detailed specifications for program requirements.
3. Design and implement programs, or modify existing programs, to meet users' requirements and to improve the efficiency and effectiveness of working processes.
4. Test programs and make any necessary modifications to ensure that they operate effectively.
5. Draw up all required support documentation for programs to ensure that users are able to operate them correctly.
6. Provide technical advice and guidance on programming matters to colleagues and system users.
7. Keep up to date with developments in programming to ensure that the company continues to take advantage of new ideas and developments.

## Knowledge, skills and experience required

The job requires:

- a degree-level education;
- a technical qualification in computing or IT;
- thorough knowledge of relevant programming languages;
- at least 3 years' experience in computer programming;
- excellent analytical skills;
- good communication skills.

# 12. SOFTWARE DESIGN MANAGER

## Main purpose of job

To lead a team of technical staff in the design and development of software which meets customers' requirements.

## Main responsibilities

1. Direct and control the staff of the team to ensure that they are appropriately motivated and trained and so that they carry out their responsibilities to the required standard.
2. Provide technical leadership in the design and development of software which meets customers' requirements.
3. Develop and implement all necessary systems and procedures to ensure that software is of the required standard.
4. Assist in the identification and development of new software applications.
5. Act as the in-house expert on all software issues and provide advice and training to company management and staff as required.
6. Represent the company as required at meetings with customers and external contractors to ensure that the software design implications of any proposals are thoroughly considered and to help maximize sales.
7. Develop a research and development programme to review all new and potential software applications.
8. Monitor and control the software development budget.
9. Maintain an awareness of developments in relation to software so that the company maintains its competitive position.

## Knowledge, skills and experience required

The job requires:

- a degree or equivalent in a relevant subject;
- at least 5 years' experience of software design;
- a thorough knowledge of relevant programming languages and operating systems;
- programming skills;

- analytical skills;
- managerial experience;
- communication and motivation skills.

# 13. SYSTEMS ANALYST

## Main purpose of job

To analyse, design and implement information technology systems and solutions to meet business, organizational and technical requirements.

## Main responsibilities

1. Identify the detailed requirements of users and clients and prepare detailed project plans for meeting these requirements.
2. Identify the various options to resolve problems and meet users' requirements and assess their suitability.
3. Prepare a detailed specification for any proposed solution.
4. Discuss any proposed solution with programmers, other technical staff and end users to ensure its technical viability and to identify any problems.
5. Test any proposed solution to ensure its effectiveness before final implementation.
6. Assist in the implementation of any new system, taking any remedial action as necessary, to ensure that it is working effectively.
7. Provide any necessary documentation and technical support following implementation to end users.
8. Train users in the new system to ensure that it continues to work effectively and to their satisfaction.

## Knowledge, skills and experience required

The job requires:

- a degree-level education;
- a technical qualification in computing;
- thorough knowledge of IT systems and systems analysis;
- good knowledge of structured systems analysis methodologies;
- at least 3 years' experience in systems analysis;
- excellent analytical skills;
- good communication skills.

# 14. WEB SITE DESIGNER

## Main purpose of job

To design and maintain the company's internal and external Web sites, and associated documents, to present a positive image of the company.

## Main responsibilities

1.  Design and develop the company's Web site to make it visually effective and easy to access.
2.  Develop and maintain the company's intranet to provide an accurate and immediate source of information to all employees.
3.  Design and distribute newsletters and other documents relating to the Web site and the intranet.
4.  Develop contacts with external providers and negotiate contracts for the design and supply of services that cannot be provided internally in relation to the Web site and intranet.
5.  Conduct presentations, internally and externally, to promote the company Web site and intranet.

## Knowledge, skills and experience required

The job requires:

*   an HNC or equivalent in a relevant subject related to design or computer applications;
*   at least 1 year's experience of Web design;
*   a thorough knowledge of relevant software packages;
*   creative skills;
*   negotiating skills;
*   programming skills;
*   good presentation and communication skills.

# 8

# Legal

This section includes job descriptions for the following jobs:

1. Assistant solicitor
2. Head of legal services
3. Legal executive
4. Principal solicitor (litigation)
5. Senior legal executive
6. Solicitor

# 1. ASSISTANT SOLICITOR

## Main purpose of job

To assist in providing legal advice and in carrying out research to support other solicitors in the team.

## Main responsibilities

1. Assist in providing accurate legal advice on less complex matters to managers and staff to ensure that decisions taken are legally correct.
2. Carry out research and prepare reports on any legal issues to support the more senior members of the team.
3. Assist in drafting legal documents on various matters, ensuring that these are legally sound and/or to ensure that the organization's interests are safeguarded.
4. Review documents to check for legal accuracy.
5. Analyse issues and problems to identify legal implications.
6. Maintain an awareness of developments in the legal field relevant to the organization, including reviewing and reporting on the implications of any new legislation.

## Knowledge, skills and experience required

The job requires:

- a qualified solicitor;
- 1–2 years' relevant post-qualification experience;
- good interpersonal skills;
- analytical skills;
- accuracy and an eye for detail.

## 2. HEAD OF LEGAL SERVICES

## Main purpose of job

To direct and control the provision of effective legal services to the company and to provide legal advice to managers and staff.

## Main responsibilities

1. Direct and control the staff of the legal services department to ensure that they are appropriately motivated and trained and that they carry out their responsibilities to the required standards.
2. Provide accurate legal advice to managers and staff to ensure that decisions taken are legally correct and that the company's interests are protected.
3. Develop and monitor an annual budget for the department to ensure that all financial targets are met and appropriate financial controls are in place.
4. Represent the company at court hearings and tribunals to ensure that the company's interests are effectively safeguarded and so that it carries out its legal obligations effectively.
5. Negotiate, and draft and implement, complex legal agreements relating to the work of the company.
6. Represent the company at meetings with external bodies to ensure that the legal aspects of any decisions are fully considered.
7. Maintain an awareness of developments in the legal field which might affect the company and prepare reports on relevant matters for consideration by management.

## Knowledge, skills and experience required

The job requires:

- a qualified solicitor with at least 10 years' post-qualification experience;
- considerable experience of advocacy;
- managerial experience;
- highly developed negotiating and interpersonal skills;
- excellent representational skills;
- thorough knowledge of the organization's work and functions.

# 3. LEGAL EXECUTIVE

## Main purpose of job

To assist in providing legal support to managers and staff so that the organization meets its legal obligations, and to protect its interests.

## Main responsibilities

1.  Assist in the preparation of all legal documents required by managers and staff to ensure that these are accurate and legally sound.
2.  Provide legal advice to managers and staff on the interpretation of statutes and legal documents to ensure that the actions they take are legally sound.
3.  Draft, review and amend legal documents drafted by, or sent to, the organization.
4.  Monitor the progress of legal transactions to ensure that the correct actions are taken at the appropriate times.
5.  Maintain an awareness of developments in all legal fields relevant to the organization.

## Knowledge, skills and experience required

The job requires:

*   a qualified legal executive;
*   at least 1 year's relevant experience;
*   up-to-date knowledge of all aspects of the law relevant to the job;
*   excellent interpersonal skills;
*   analytical skills;
*   accuracy and an eye for detail.

# 4. PRINCIPAL SOLICITOR (LITIGATION)

## Main purpose of job

To direct and control litigation services to ensure that the organization carries out its legal obligations and to protect its interests.

## Main responsibilities

1.  Provide accurate legal advice to managers and staff to ensure that decisions taken are legally correct.
2.  Represent the organization at court hearings and tribunals to ensure that the organization's interests are effectively safeguarded and so that it carries out its legal obligations effectively.
3.  Assist in organizing and controlling the work of the department to ensure that staff are appropriately trained and motivated and carry out their responsibilities to the required standards.
4.  Represent the organization at meetings with external bodies to ensure that the legal aspects of any decisions are fully considered.
5.  Carry out research and prepare reports on any legally complex issues to ensure that the organization has full information about the legal implications of any decisions.
6.  Undertake any required litigation to protect the interests of the organization.
7.  Maintain an awareness of developments in the legal field which might affect the organization and prepare reports on relevant matters for consideration by management.

## Knowledge, skills and experience required

The job requires:

*   a qualified solicitor with at least 5 years' post-qualification experience;
*   considerable experience of advocacy;
*   managerial skills;
*   highly developed negotiating and interpersonal skills;
*   thorough knowledge of the organization's work and functions.

## 5. SENIOR LEGAL EXECUTIVE

## Main purpose of job

To supervise the provision of legal support to managers and staff so that the organization meets its legal obligations, and to protect its interests.

## Main responsibilities

1. Supervise legal staff to ensure that they carry out their responsibilities to the required standards and receive all necessary training and development.
2. Assist in the preparation of all legal documents required by managers and staff to ensure that these are accurate and legally sound.
3. Provide legal advice to managers and staff on the interpretation of statutes and legal documents to ensure that the actions they take are legally sound.
4. Represent the organization at courts and tribunals on routine matters to ensure that the organization's interests are safeguarded.
5. Draft, review and amend legal documents drafted by, or sent to, the organization.
6. Monitor the progress of legal transactions to ensure that the correct actions are taken at the appropriate times.
7. Instruct counsel where necessary.
8. Maintain an awareness of developments in all legal fields relevant to the organization.

## Knowledge, skills and experience required

The job requires:

- a qualified legal executive;
- at least 3 years' relevant experience;
- up-to-date knowledge of all aspects of the law relevant to the job;
- supervisory skills;
- excellent interpersonal skills;
- analytical skills;
- accuracy and an eye for detail;
- excellent presentation skills.

# 6. SOLICITOR

## Main purpose of job

To assist in providing legal services to ensure that the organization carries out its statutory obligations, and to protect its interests.

## Main responsibilities

1. Provide accurate legal advice within a specific area to managers and staff to ensure that decisions taken are legally correct.
2. Represent the organization at routine court hearings and tribunals to ensure that the organization's interests are effectively safeguarded and so that it carries out its legal obligations effectively.
3. Supervise the work of legal executives to ensure that they are appropriately trained and motivated and carry out their responsibilities to the required standards.
4. Represent the organization at meetings with external bodies on specific topics to ensure that the legal aspects of any decisions are fully considered.
5. Carry out research and prepare reports on any legally complex issues to ensure that the organization has full information about the legal implications of any decisions.
6. Draft and review complex legal documents on various matters, ensuring that these are legally sound and/or to ensure that the organization's interests are safeguarded.
7. Maintain an awareness of developments in the legal field relevant to the organization, including reviewing and reporting on the implications of any new legislation.

## Knowledge, skills and experience required

The job requires:

- a qualified solicitor;
- experience of advocacy;
- supervisory skills;
- highly developed negotiating and interpersonal skills;
- analytical skills;
- accuracy and an eye for detail;
- excellent presentation skills.

# 9

# Leisure services

This section includes job descriptions for the following jobs:

1. Administrative assistant
2. Leisure centre manager
3. Pool attendant
4. Recreation assistant

# 1. ADMINISTRATIVE ASSISTANT

## Main purpose of job

To provide administrative support in the running of a leisure centre.

## Main responsibilities

1. Provide counter and cash collection services to members of the public and maintain records of the centre's income and expenditure.
2. Maintain all financial and staffing records, including staff time-sheets.
3. Process applications for membership and maintain the computerized membership records system.
4. Maintain up-to-date records of centre activities and provide information to members of the public on these.
5. Process all invoices, claim forms, timesheets, bills etc.
6. Type reports and letters as required.
7. Produce and maintain all necessary documents to publicize centre activities and give advice on the use of equipment.
8. Carry out a range of routine clerical activities, including opening post, sending out routine replies, photocopying, compiling membership records etc.

## Knowledge, skills and experience required

The job requires:

- education to A-level standard;
- good word processing and keyboard skills;
- knowledge of word processing and spreadsheet applications;
- good numeracy and literacy;
- experience of office procedures;
- organizational ability;
- excellent interpersonal skills and experience of dealing with the public.

# 2. LEISURE CENTRE MANAGER

## Main purpose of job

To be responsible for the day-to-day running of the leisure centre to ensure that customers receive the best possible service consistent with meeting the company's financial targets.

## Main responsibilities

1. Supervise the staff of the centre to ensure that they receive all necessary training and instruction and carry out their responsibilities to the required standards.
2. Develop and implement all necessary procedures to ensure that the centre runs smoothly.
3. Monitor and control all budgets and cash to ensure that the centre meets all established financial targets.
4. Maintain a liaison with members of the public and all the users of the centre to ensure that they receive the best possible customer care.
5. Develop and implement centre activities identified by market research and agreed to as part of the business plan.
6. Monitor and review existing activities to ensure that they meet identified customer requirements.
7. Monitor all centre activities to ensure that they comply with health and safety requirements in relation to both staff and customers.
8. Take any necessary steps to ensure that the security of the building is maintained to the highest standards.
9. Supervise cleaners and other contractors to ensure that work is carried out to the required standards.

## Knowledge, skills and experience required

The job requires:

- qualification to graduate level;
- at least 3 years' experience in the field of leisure and recreation management;
- supervisory experience;

- knowledge of health and safety issues relating to leisure centres;
- excellent organizational skills;
- excellent interpersonal skills.

# 3. POOL ATTENDANT

## Main purpose of job

To supervise, support and assist members of the general public when using pool facilities and to ensure that standards of health and safety are maintained.

## Main responsibilities

1.  Patrol the swimming pool to ensure that the facilities and equipment are used correctly and safely.
2.  Instruct members of the public in the use of the swimming pool and associated equipment as necessary.
3.  Operate the pool control system.
4.  Erect, adjust and dismantle equipment as required.
5.  Provide assistance and respond to inquiries from the public as necessary.
6.  Clean equipment, changing rooms and other facilities to promote high standards of hygiene.

## Knowledge, skills and experience required

The job requires:

- a strong swimmer;
- an ability to teach swimming;
- ideally, qualifications in recreation or sports coaching;
- previous experience of dealing with the public;
- experience of organizing sports events;
- flexibility and initiative.

## 4. RECREATION ASSISTANT

## Main purpose of job

To supervise, support and assist members of the general public when using leisure centre facilities and to ensure that standards of health and safety are maintained.

## Main responsibilities

1. Patrol gymnasium and other leisure facilities to ensure that equipment and other facilities are used correctly and safely.
2. Instruct members of the public in the use of equipment as necessary.
3. Erect, adjust and dismantle equipment as required.
4. Provide assistance and respond to enquiries from the public as necessary.
5. Clean equipment, changing rooms and other facilities to promote high standards of hygiene.

## Knowledge, skills and experience required

The job requires:

- ideally, qualifications in recreation or sports coaching;
- previous experience of dealing with the public;
- knowledge of how to use sports equipment;
- experience of organizing sports events;
- flexibility and initiative.

# 10

# Public relations and media

This section includes job descriptions for the following jobs:

1. Commissioning editor
2. Communications executive
3. Desk editor
4. Editor
5. Marketing executive
6. Media coordinator
7. Press officer
8. Production manager
9. Public relations director
10. Public relations manager
11. Public relations officer
12. Publicity executive
13. Publishing director
14. Sales manager (publishing)

# 1. COMMISSIONING EDITOR

## Main purpose of job

To develop a list of publications in defined market sectors to develop, increase and maintain the company's market share and monitor and review progress to ensure that they are produced to budget and schedule and are appropriately prepared for the target market.

## Main responsibilities

1.  Commission an agreed number of new titles and/or new editions in defined subject areas each year to meet agreed targets.
2.  Maintain backlist through new editions and reprints.
3.  Identify any gaps in the market and approach appropriate authors to help fill those gaps.
4.  Read and assess the suitability of unsolicited scripts and/or proposals.
5.  Research the marketability and sales potential of proposals and/or scripts and prepare a report to the publishing committee.
6.  Negotiate contracts with authors and agree style and content of publications.
7.  Monitor and review progress on publications to ensure that schedules and budget targets are met.
8.  Arrange for final script to be vetted by appropriate experts, consult author on proposed changes, prepare for publication and ensure that all those involved in the editorial and production process are kept informed of developments.
9.  Make all necessary arrangements relating to the style, design of text and cover for the publication, within agreed budget limits.
10. Assist with marketing the publication in the UK and overseas and develop list of useful contacts.
11. Maintain regular contact with all departments involved in the publishing process to ensure effective coordination.

## Knowledge, skills and experience required

The job requires:

- degree or equivalent;
- at least 3 years' experience in publishing;
- thorough knowledge of the market;
- excellent DTP knowledge;
- excellent copywriting skills;
- research skills;
- commercial awareness;
- excellent interpersonal and persuasive skills.

# 2. COMMUNICATIONS EXECUTIVE

## Main purpose of job

To assist in the production and distribution of publications and other media to publicize the organization's activities and promote a positive brand image.

## Main responsibilities

1. Produce and distribute printed material and other media to publicize the organization's activities and to provide information and guidance.
2. Write copy and read proofs for publications and print media as required.
3. Maintain the photograph, media and video library to provide a comprehensive source of information about the organization.
4. Develop and maintain a network of internal contacts to keep abreast of developments in the organization and to ensure that employees are aware of the organization's activities, objectives and corporate image.
5. Carry out general administrative duties in support of the section, including replying to routine correspondence.

## Knowledge, skills and experience required

The job requires:

- education to GCSE level;
- at least 12 months' office experience;
- written communication skills;
- organizational skills;
- good interpersonal skills.

## 3. DESK EDITOR

## Main purpose of job

To oversee all stages of the production of manuscripts and reprints, maintaining a constant liaison with the author, commissioning editor and production department as necessary.

## Main responsibilities

1. Monitor all stages of the production process to ensure that the production schedule is adhered to.
2. Maintain the reprints file and keep the production department informed of any changes necessary.
3. Maintain regular contact with authors to ensure that any minor amendments or corrections required by them are collated and implemented.
4. Carry out proof-reading to ensure a high standard of accuracy in texts sent for production.
5. Prepare manuscripts for editing.
6. Commission and brief freelance copy editors and proof-readers and send proofs to authors for checking.
7. Organize, edit and proof-read the index for each publication.

## Knowledge, skills and experience required

The job requires:

- degree or equivalent;
- at least 2 years' experience in publishing;
- excellent DTP knowledge;
- excellent copywriting and proof-reading skills;
- commercial awareness;
- excellent interpersonal and persuasive skills.

## 4. EDITOR

## Main purpose of job

To edit and prepare documents for publication to agreed deadlines and standards.

## Main responsibilities

1. Advise authors on the content and presentation of items for publication to ensure that they are of the required standard and are produced at the right time.
2. Develop any required processes and procedures to ensure that publications are produced to the right standards to agreed deadlines.
3. Control the process for the production of publications, maintaining regular contact with external designers and printers, to ensure that publications are produced to the required standards and within agreed deadlines.
4. Edit publications to ensure that they conform to a high standard of grammar and presentation.
5. Research and draft articles for publication.
6. Maintain any necessary records relating to the production and control of publications.

## Knowledge, skills and experience required

The job requires:

- qualification to degree level;
- at least 2 years' editing experience;
- detailed knowledge of publishing software;
- well-developed proof-reading skills;
- writing skills;
- computer skills;
- good interpersonal skills;
- excellent time management skills.

# 5. MARKETING EXECUTIVE

## Main purpose of job

To promote the sales of books and publications by applying a range of marketing techniques.

## Main responsibilities

1. Plan marketing campaigns for new books and publications to maximize sales.
2. Establish and maintain contacts with the publisher, editor and other internal staff to assist in the planning of marketing campaigns for the publications they are associated with.
3. Control the production and distribution of promotional material within agreed budget limits.
4. Commission and brief external contractors in the design and production of promotional material.
5. Analyse the results of marketing campaigns and make whatever changes may be required to improve sales performance.
6. Design and produce marketing material to promote sales of specific publications.
7. Prepare and distribute press releases and organize and attend book launches and conferences for specific publications.
8. Develop and maintain a range of external contacts with organizations and individuals who can assist in the sales and marketing of publications.

## Knowledge, skills and experience required

The job requires:

- qualification to degree level;
- at least 2 years' marketing experience;
- thorough knowledge of the publications being marketed;
- excellent interpersonal and communication skills;
- selling skills;
- public relations and marketing skills;
- writing skills;
- financial awareness.

## 6. MEDIA COORDINATOR

## Main purpose of job

To design and produce all printed publicity material to agreed corporate standards to promote the image of the organization.

## Main responsibilities

1. Identify appropriate materials for the production of designs and printed matter.
2. Draft copy in consultation with other staff for inclusion in brochures, newsletters and other internal and external publications.
3. Commission photographers and designers and brief them on house style to enable them to produce artwork of the standard required.
4. Produce detailed specifications for all work contracted out and negotiate cost-effective contracts with suppliers.
5. Maintain a list of preferred suppliers to ensure that the organization gets the best value for money.
6. Control the process for the production of publications to ensure that they are produced to the required standards and at the right time.
7. Proof-read publications to ensure that they are accurate and that the design and layout meets corporate standards.
8. Advise managers and staff on the design, presentation and cost-effectiveness of their print requirements.
9. Maintain a good working knowledge of production processes, DTP computer systems, photography, papers and other materials, to be able to provide an internal source of expertise and to monitor the quality of work carried out by external suppliers.

## Knowledge, skills and experience required

The job requires:

- qualification to GCSE level;
- at least 2 years' experience in DTP, printing or a related field;
- good design skills;
- accuracy;
- good project and time management skills.

# 7. PRESS OFFICER

## Main purpose of job

To act as a point of contact for media enquiries, creating opportunities for media coverage of the organization's work and handling crisis situations as they arise.

## Main responsibilities

1. Respond to press and media enquiries to provide information and to ensure that the organization's view is effectively presented.
2. Develop news items and stories to describe the organization's products and services.
3. Draft press releases and letters to promote the organization's policies and views.
4. Maintain a list of press and media contacts to ensure that they are kept informed of the organization's policies and activities.
5. Attend press conferences and briefings to maintain an awareness of key issues and to respond to enquiries.
6. Monitor media articles to ensure that the organization is kept aware of issues of significance.

## Knowledge, skills and experience required

The job requires:

- education to graduate level or a suitable PR or marketing qualification;
- at least 2 years' PR/corporate communications experience;
- thorough understanding of the work of the organization and related bodies;
- excellent interpersonal skills.

# 8. PRODUCTION MANAGER

## Main purpose of job

To oversee all stages of the production process, ensuring that publications are produced at the appropriate time, to the required standards and within agreed budgets.

## Main responsibilities

1.  Oversee all stages of the production process to ensure that publications are produced on time to the required standards and within budget.
2.  Develop production plans for all publications and establish costs for each stage to ensure the effective management and control of the production process.
3.  Provide technical advice on all aspects of the production process to company staff and external contractors so that they are fully aware of production requirements.
4.  Develop and maintain contacts with external suppliers and negotiate the most favourable terms for the company to keep production costs to the minimum.
5.  Investigate potential new suppliers to ensure that the company takes advantage of the best available rates.
6.  Purchase all required materials for the production process, negotiating the most favourable terms for the company.
7.  Research and implement technical developments in the production process and consult company staff on proposed changes to improve the overall efficiency and effectiveness of the process.

## Knowledge, skills and experience required

The job requires:

- qualification to degree level;
- at least 3 years' experience of book production;
- detailed knowledge of the publishing process and production techniques;
- excellent organizational skills;

- computer skills;
- good interpersonal and negotiating skills;
- excellent time management skills.

# 9. PUBLIC RELATIONS DIRECTOR

## Main purpose of job

To direct and control the public relations function and give strategic advice to the managers and staff in their dealings with the media, so that a positive public image of the organization is promoted.

## Main responsibilities

1.   Direct and control the staff of the Public Relations Department to ensure that they achieve their objectives and receive all appropriate training and development.
2.   Give strategic advice to the managers and staff in relation to their dealings with the media, to promote the public profile of the organization.
3.   Develop and implement the organization's public relations and communications strategy to ensure the best publicity for the organization.
4.   Develop and maintain contacts with national, local and specialist media to maximize PR opportunities, to promote the organization's activities and events, and to minimize negative publicity.
5.   Develop an internal communications network to ensure that all staff are kept informed of the organization's policies and achievements and to get source material for publicity purposes.
6.   Develop and monitor the department's budget to ensure that the necessary financial resources are made available and that expenditure is kept within the prescribed limits.
7.   Direct and monitor external projects to ensure that activities are carried out to the required standard, within agreed budgets, and that targets are met.
8.   Consult with external agencies in the planning and execution of events to ensure effective organization representation, to maximize PR opportunities and to ensure that they meet their obligations.
9.   Oversee the development and maintenance of the photograph library, Web site, publications and other communications/marketing tools.
10.   Maintain an awareness of developments in the field of public relations.

## Knowledge, skills and experience required

The job requires:

- qualification to degree level;
- ideally a relevant professional qualification;
- at least 10 years' relevant PR or corporate communications experience;
- thorough understanding of the work of the organization;
- substantial experience of managing people and budgets;
- excellent interpersonal and communication skills;
- writing skills.

## 10. PUBLIC RELATIONS MANAGER

## Main purpose of job

To promote the public image of the organization through advertising, direct marketing and any other appropriate PR techniques.

## Main responsibilities

1.  Develop policies and processes which directly contribute to the promotion of the organization's public image.
2.  Supervise Public Relations staff to ensure that they are appropriately motivated and trained and carry out their responsibilities to the required standards.
3.  Develop and direct campaigns for the promotion of the organization's policies.
4.  Develop a media relations programme with appropriate print and broadcast media to raise awareness of the organization and its policies.
5.  Develop and maintain effective contacts with a wide range of external bodies, including contractors and suppliers, to ensure wide publicity and cost-effective support for the organization's policies and activities.
6.  Develop a range of publications to promote the organization and its policies.
7.  Draft press releases and articles for publication to promote the image of the organization.
8.  Negotiate contracts with suppliers for any services which cannot be provided in-house and monitor performance to ensure that they are of the standard required.
9.  Monitor the department's budget to ensure that services provided are within agreed financial limits.
10. Provide expertise and advice to managers and staff on all matters with public relations implications.
11. Keep abreast of developments within the field of public relations to ensure that the organization maintains the highest standards of public relations.

## Knowledge, skills and experience required

The job requires:

- qualification to degree level;
- at least 5 years' experience in public relations;
- excellent contacts in the media and government;
- good knowledge of the organization;
- managerial experience;
- excellent interpersonal skills.

# 11. PUBLIC RELATIONS OFFICER

## Main purpose of job

To assist in the implementation of policies which help to give a positive image of the organization to external bodies.

## Main responsibilities

1. Establish and maintain a press office for the organization which will provide a database of media information to be used in the promotion of the organization's aims and objectives.
2. Assist in the production of publications to promote the image of the organization.
3. Respond to enquiries from the media to ensure that a positive image of the organization is promoted.
4. Assist in drafting press releases to promote the aims and objectives of the organization.
5. Assist in maintaining the Web site to ensure that it remains up to date, informative and interesting.
6. Assist in organizing events to promote the image, aims and objectives of the organization.
7. Maintain a network of contacts internally and externally to ensure that positive information about the organization is obtained and promulgated.
8. Provide advice and support on public relations issues to managers and staff to ensure that a positive image of the organization is promoted.

## Knowledge, skills and experience required

The job requires:

- qualification to degree level;
- at least 2 years' experience in public relations;
- good knowledge of the organization;
- excellent interpersonal skills;
- good verbal and written communication skills.

## 12. PUBLICITY EXECUTIVE

## Main purpose of job

To act as the organization's first point of contact for media enquiries, and to create opportunities for media coverage of the organization's activities and services.

## Main responsibilities

1.  Research and develop news items and stories about the organization's activities and services to promote a positive image of the organization and to raise its profile.
2.  Respond to questions and issues raised about the organization and its activities to ensure that the organization's viewpoint is accurately and effectively presented.
3.  Draft press releases and letters to promote the organization's viewpoint.
4.  Compile and maintain a list of press and media contacts and of relevant events to ensure that the organization has up-to-date information.
5.  Attend press conferences and briefings to maintain an awareness of key issues.
6.  Organize the supply of the organization's publicity materials to ensure maximum publicity at events.
7.  Research and prepare briefing notes to ensure that managers have all relevant information when addressing press and media enquiries.
8.  Maintain regular contact with members of the media to ensure the positive coverage and promotion of the organization's activities and services and to respond to any issues arising.

## Knowledge, skills and experience required

The job requires:

- qualification to degree level;
- at least 2 years' relevant experience;
- thorough understanding of the work of the organization;
- excellent interpersonal and communication skills;
- writing skills.

# 13. PUBLISHING DIRECTOR

## Main purpose of job

To direct and control the publishing function and to develop and implement the publishing strategy to ensure the achievement of the company's corporate objectives.

## Main responsibilities

1. Direct and control the staff of the publishing function to ensure that they achieve their objectives and receive all appropriate training and development.
2. Develop and implement the company's publishing strategy to ensure the achievement of the company's corporate objectives and to maximize revenues from the sale of publications.
3. Develop and maintain a range of contacts with authors, book-sellers and other members of the book trade to promote the development and sales of the company's products.
4. Attend meetings, conferences etc to promote the image and reputation of the company and to develop business.
5. Develop and monitor the department's budget to ensure that the necessary financial resources are made available and that expenditure is kept within the prescribed limits.
6. Negotiate contracts with suppliers for any services which cannot be provided in-house and monitor performance to ensure that they are of the standard required.
7. Direct and control the production process to ensure that publications are produced on time to the required standards and within budget.
8. Direct and monitor external projects to ensure that activities are carried out to the required standard, within agreed budgets, and that targets are met.
9. Maintain an awareness of developments in the field of publishing and in competitor activity to ensure that the company maintains and improves its competitive position.

## Knowledge, skills and experience required

The job requires:

- qualification to degree level;
- ideally a relevant professional qualification;
- at least 10 years' relevant publishing experience;
- thorough understanding of the work of the company;
- substantial experience of managing people and budgets;
- excellent interpersonal and communication skills;
- writing skills.

## 14. SALES MANAGER (PUBLISHING)

## Main purpose of job

To maximize revenue from sales of publications.

## Main responsibilities

1.  Develop policies and procedures to maximize revenues from the sale of publications.
2.  Develop and maintain a network of sales representatives and allocate them budgets and targets for the sale of company publications.
3.  Develop and monitor budgets for sales representatives and for advertising and conferences to ensure that these deliver the results required.
4.  Oversee the organization of sales conferences, sales meetings and other sales promotions to ensure that company products are effectively promoted.
5.  Oversee key accounts to keep them informed of publications and to maximize sales.
6.  Visit booksellers and other outlets to promote company publications.
7.  Maintain up-to-date knowledge of developments in the book trade and keep colleagues informed of these so that the company maintains its competitive position.

## Knowledge, skills and experience required

The job requires:

- qualification to degree level;
- at least 2 years' experience of publishing sales;
- thorough knowledge of the publications being sold;
- excellent interpersonal and communication skills;
- selling skills;
- public relations and marketing skills;
- financial awareness.

# 11

# Purchasing and stores

This section includes job descriptions for the following jobs:

1. Buyer
2. Materials controller
3. Purchasing manager
4. Stores manager

# 1. BUYER

## Main purpose of job

To purchase materials and equipment required by the company at the optimum quality and price to meet operational and customer requirements.

## Main responsibilities

1. Negotiate the purchase of materials and equipment required by the company, ensuring that these meet specifications and can be delivered at the correct time at the most favourable prices.
2. Monitor purchase orders to ensure that these are modified to meet changes in requirements.
3. Maintain up-to-date lists of contractors and pricing arrangements to ensure that the company achieves the most favourable commercial terms.
4. Monitor the performance of suppliers and products to ensure that they meet the required standards.
5. Maintain an awareness of quantities of stocks of materials and equipment to ensure that shortages are avoided.
6. Monitor the purchasing arrangements of different departments and functions to ensure that they are taking advantage of the most favourable terms.
7. Report any significant supply problems to ensure that departments and functions are kept aware of any potential difficulties.

## Knowledge, skills and experience required

The job requires:

- an appropriate purchasing qualification;
- at least 2 years' experience in the purchasing function;
- thorough knowledge of company products;
- excellent negotiating skills.

# 2. MATERIALS CONTROLLER

## Main purpose of job

To control the purchase of all materials for the company to ensure that they are in accordance with specification and price.

## Main responsibilities

1. Place orders for all required materials to ensure that all such purchases are delivered at the appropriate time and in accordance with company requirements.
2. Monitor all purchase orders to ensure that materials are delivered on time and to specification.
3. Monitor the costs of materials purchased to ensure that these comply with the company's cost criteria and to maximize savings to the company.
4. Negotiate contract and price terms with suppliers to maximize savings to the company.
5. Monitor the performance of suppliers and subcontractors to ensure that the company continues to use those providing the best service.
6. Compile and maintain a list of preferred and non-approved suppliers and subcontractors.
7. Maintain a comprehensive database relating to materials and suppliers to ensure that the company has accurate and up-to-date information.
8. Prepare regular reports on materials and supplier performance to assist in decision making.

## Knowledge, skills and experience required

The job requires:

- secondary-level education;
- a purchasing qualification;
- a minimum of 1 year's experience of working in purchasing;
- knowledge of the industry;
- excellent negotiating skills.

# 3. PURCHASING MANAGER

## Main purpose of job

To direct and control the central purchasing function to ensure that goods and supplies are purchased at the most competitive prices and are of the required quality.

## Main responsibilities

1. Direct and control purchasing staff to ensure that they are well motivated and trained and that they carry out their responsibilities to the required standards.
2. Assist in the development of a central purchasing policy to ensure that the company makes the best use of its purchasing power.
3. Negotiate contracts with suppliers who meet the company's requirements to secure the most favourable terms of business for the company.
4. Develop and implement all necessary policies and procedures to ensure that the purchasing function operates effectively.
5. Keep all contracts for the supply of goods and services under review to ensure that they are being carried out effectively and renegotiate terms where necessary.
6. Maintain the central purchasing budget to ensure the effective monitoring and control of all purchases.
7. Maintain an awareness of any developments in the field of central purchasing or with suppliers to ensure that the company continues to apply the most effective policies and procedures.
8. Act as the company's adviser on all matters relating to the purchasing function.

## Knowledge, skills and experience required

The job requires:

- qualifications equivalent to a degree or NVQ4 in an appropriate discipline;
- at least 5 years' experience in a central purchasing function;
- managerial experience;

- experience of managing budgets;
- excellent negotiating skills;
- good communication skills;
- good interpersonal skills.

# 4. STORES MANAGER

## Main purpose of job

To manage the company's stores to ensure that all parts and other stock are available as required.

## Main responsibilities

1. Maintain adequate supplies of parts and materials to meet production requirements.
2. Issue parts, materials and equipment from stores as required.
3. Receive replacement stocks of parts, materials and equipment, ensuring that these are correct in terms of number and specification.
4. Maintain up-to-date records of all stock movements to ensure that optimum stock levels are maintained.
5. Carry out regular stock checks to ensure that adequate supplies are maintained.
6. Reorder stock as required to ensure that the optimum levels of required parts, materials and equipment are maintained.
7. Maintain a tidy, safe and efficient stores environment.
8. Maintain contact with relevant departments to ensure that stock items and stock levels are appropriate to their requirements.

## Knowledge, skills and experience required

The job requires:

- secondary-level education;
- a minimum of 6 months' experience of working in stores and of stock control;
- knowledge of the industry;
- good organizing skills.

# 12

# Research and development (R&D) and science

This section includes job descriptions for the following jobs:

1. Analytical chemist
2. Archaeologist
3. Biologist
4. Business development manager
5. Chief pharmacist
6. Economist
7. Geologist
8. Laboratory technician
9. Microbiologist
10. Pharmacist
11. Product development manager
12. R&D director
13. Research manager
14. Researcher
15. Senior economist
16. Statistician

# 1. ANALYTICAL CHEMIST

## Main purpose of job

To analyse substances, using various analytical techniques and instruments to determine their chemical content.

## Main responsibilities

1. Analyse samples of substances, using various analytical techniques and instruments to determine their chemical content.
2. Set up and maintain instrumentation for experimental, demonstration or other purposes.
3. Prepare and analyse fluids, secretions and/or tissue to detect infections or to examine the effects of different substances.
4. Grow and prepare cultures of bacteria and viruses, tissue sections and other organic and inorganic material and fix slides for examination by microscope and other processes.
5. Carry out measurements and analyses and ensure that sterile conditions necessary for some equipment are maintained.
6. Record and collate data from chemical analysis work and document all work carried out.
7. Establish and maintain contacts within the organization and with external customers to acquire information and to ensure that they are kept informed of relevant developments.
8. Keep up to date with developments in chemical analysis to ensure that the latest techniques and instrumentation are used.
9. Observe all requirements to maintain a safe and healthy working environment.

## Knowledge, skills and experience required

The job requires:

- a good degree in chemistry;
- ideally a relevant higher degree;
- at least 3 years' experience of chemical analysis;
- thorough knowledge of analytical techniques and instrumentation;

- knowledge of health and safety in a laboratory environment;
- accuracy;
- good communication skills.

# 2. ARCHAEOLOGIST

## Main purpose of job

To survey and excavate archaeological sites and analyse findings to reconstruct earlier cultures and histories and determine their importance.

## Main responsibilities

1. Survey and excavate archaeological sites and record and catalogue all items found.
2. Analyse survey findings to reconstruct earlier cultures, study their history and determine their historical importance and impact on modern life.
3. Identify, reconstruct and classify findings from archaeological sites.
4. Carry out research into findings and publish these to improve knowledge of the culture in question.
5. Oversee the preservation of archaeological sites and assist in providing information about these.
6. Carry out lectures and presentations and generally disseminate information about cultures researched.
7. Observe all requirements to maintain a safe and healthy working environment.

## Knowledge, skills and experience required

The job requires:

- higher degree in a related scientific field;
- relevant survey and excavation experience;
- research and analysis skills;
- organization skills;
- presentation skills.

273

# 3. BIOLOGIST

## Main purpose of job

To carry out biological research using a range of diagnostic methods and to record results obtained.

## Main responsibilities

1. Carry out the routine microscopic analysis of samples and record and interpret the results obtained.
2. Determine the appropriate methods and equipment required for the effective analysis and examination of samples.
3. Carry out research and prepare reports and scientific papers relating to research findings.
4. Maintain a liaison with staff, customers and relevant external bodies to obtain information and report on research findings.
5. Develop and monitor processes to ensure effective quality assurance within the laboratory and for maintaining accreditation with relevant agencies.
6. Maintain all necessary records ensuring confidentiality and compliance with the Data Protection Act.
7. Maintain an up-to-date knowledge of developments in the field of biological research.
8. Observe all requirements to maintain a safe and healthy working environment.

## Knowledge, skills and experience required

The job requires:

- a relevant science degree;
- a relevant higher degree;
- at least 3 years' experience of biological research;
- analytical skills;
- research skills;
- good written and verbal communication skills.

# 4. BUSINESS DEVELOPMENT MANAGER

## Main purpose of job

To identify and develop new business opportunities which will help the company achieve its strategic and business objectives.

## Main responsibilities

1. Develop and implement information systems which will provide data on existing and potential customers to enable the company to identify opportunities for new sales.
2. Develop and implement systems and processes to enable the effective monitoring of performance and the identification of improvements in product quality and service delivery.
3. Carry out or commission surveys of customer satisfaction to identify the scope for improvements in product quality and service delivery.
4. Carry out or commission research in the company's existing and potential markets to identify new opportunities.
5. Assist other departments in the risk assessment of new products and services.
6. Assist in the development of sales and marketing literature and associated documents to improve the marketing of the company and its products.
7. Provide the main source of expertise to the company on business development issues.
8. Maintain regular contact with the sales and production functions to keep abreast of any developments in products and services.
9. Maintain an awareness of developments in the fields of product marketing and research to ensure that the company continues to compete effectively.

## Knowledge, skills and experience required

The job requires:

- education to degree level or equivalent;
- at least 5 years' experience in marketing and market research;

- thorough knowledge of company products and services;
- research and analysis skills;
- good interpersonal skills.

# 5. CHIEF PHARMACIST

## Main purpose of job

To direct and control a team of pharmacists in the provision of full dispensary services, ensuring that medicines and drugs are correctly dispensed and that all dispensary procedures, guidelines, legal and medical requirements are followed.

## Main purpose of job

1. Direct, organize and train the pharmacists working in the dispensary to ensure that the dispensary operates effectively and that all staff perform their duties to the required standards.
2. Monitor the workload in the dispensary, taking any necessary action to ensure that all outputs are achieved to the required standards.
3. Dispense drugs and medicines as required in accordance with agreed procedures and guidelines.
4. Develop and implement all necessary procedures and guidelines to ensure the effective dispensing and control of drugs and medicines and monitor these to ensure that they are kept up to date.
5. Give professional pharmaceutical advice to medical and professional staff and customers.
6. Oversee the maintenance of all required records relating to the issues of drugs and medicines and ensure that these are kept confidential.
7. Take all necessary steps to ensure that drugs and medicines are stored securely and in the right conditions.
8. Develop and maintain all necessary procedures and controls to ensure that health, safety and other statutory requirements are complied with.
9. Maintain up-to-date knowledge of drugs and medicines and pharmacy practice to ensure that services provided are of the highest standard.

## Knowledge, skills and experience required

The job requires:

- a degree in pharmacy;
- membership of the Royal Pharmaceutical Society;
- further clinical qualifications;
- at least 3 years' experience of working in a pharmacy;
- managerial experience;
- experience of drug monitoring;
- excellent interpersonal skills and experience of patient counselling;
- excellent communication skills;
- training skills.

# 6. ECONOMIST

## Main purpose of job

To carry out economic research and analysis and provide a source of economic expertise and advice to support the development of strategy and policies.

## Main responsibilities

1.  Carry out economic research and analysis in identified markets and communicate results to managers to assist in effective policy development and decision making.
2.  Maintain and develop a comprehensive and up-to-date knowledge of economic developments in the sector to ensure that any analysis carried out is based on the best and most up-to-date information.
3.  Respond to enquiries from managers and relevant external bodies relating to economic developments in the organization and the sector.
4.  Produce regular publications and use a variety of communications to ensure that managers and staff are kept up to date with economic developments relevant to their jobs.
5.  Develop and maintain contacts with external sources to ensure that the best possible information is gained and to provide effective advice to managers and staff.
6.  Represent the organization at external meetings and conferences on economic issues, ensuring that a positive image of the organization is promoted.
7.  Maintain a comprehensive database of relevant economic information.

## Knowledge, skills and experience required

The job requires:

- a good economics degree;
- ideally a higher degree in economics or a related subject;
- at least 3 years' experience in economic analysis and research;

- thorough knowledge of the sector;
- thorough knowledge of company products and services;
- research and analysis skills;
- good interpersonal skills.

# 7. GEOLOGIST

## Main purpose of job

To study and analyse the nature and composition of soils, rocks and groundwater to determine their suitability for construction projects and to advise on suitable materials and construction processes.

## Main responsibilities

1. Study sites through the use of geological maps and aerial photographs to determine their suitability for construction projects.
2. Carry out detailed field investigations through taking and analysing soil samples to identify construction requirements.
3. Determine and advise on suitable materials and processes to achieve sound and durable structures.
4. Prepare reports advising on findings to engineers and others involved in construction projects.
5. Advise on specific geological problems and suggest solutions.
6. Assist in analysing the costs associated with construction projects.
7. Maintain an up-to-date knowledge of developments in the geological field to ensure that decisions are based on the latest information and techniques.

## Knowledge, skills and experience required

The job requires:

- a degree in geology;
- at least 3 years' experience of geological research;
- analytical skills;
- an ability to write and present clear reports;
- good interpersonal skills;
- good communication skills.

# 8. LABORATORY TECHNICIAN

## Main purpose of job

To carry out routine laboratory tests and provide technical support to scientists or researchers undertaking research, development, analysis and testing.

## Main responsibilities

1. Set up scientific apparatus and prepare laboratory for experimental, demonstration or other purposes.
2. Carry out routine testing in accordance with instructions, using specialized scientific equipment.
3. Prepare and analyse fluids, secretions and/or tissue to detect infections or to examine the effects of different drugs.
4. Grow and prepare cultures of bacteria and viruses, tissue sections and other organic and inorganic material and fix slides for examination by microscope and other processes.
5. Carry out prescribed measurements and analyses and ensure that sterile conditions necessary for some equipment are maintained.
6. Record and collate data from experimental work and document all work carried out.
7. Observe all requirements to maintain a safe and healthy working environment.

## Knowledge, skills and experience required

The job requires:

- a degree in a science subject;
- at least 1 year's experience of laboratory work;
- good knowledge of laboratory techniques and processes;
- knowledge of health and safety in a laboratory environment;
- accuracy.

# 9. MICROBIOLOGIST

## Main purpose of job

To analyse micro-organisms using a range of diagnostic methods and to record results obtained.

## Main responsibilities

1. Examine the physical and chemical form, structure and composition of micro-organisms and record and interpret the results obtained.
2. Examine and record the chemical substances involved in physiological processes and infections.
3. Carry out blood tests to study physiological and pathological characteristics of blood cells.
4. Determine the appropriate methods and equipment required for the effective examination of micro-organisms.
5. Maintain a liaison with staff and relevant external bodies relating to the diagnosis and prevention of infection.
6. Develop and monitor processes to ensure effective quality assurance within the laboratory and for maintaining accreditation with relevant agencies.
7. Advise on the development of policies relating to antibiotics, use of disinfectants and infection control.
8. Maintain all necessary records ensuring confidentiality and compliance with the Data Protection Act.
9. Carry out research as required.
10. Maintain an up-to-date knowledge of developments in the field of microbiology.
11. Observe all requirements to maintain a safe and healthy working environment.

## Knowledge, skills and experience required

The job requires:

- a relevant science degree;
- a relevant higher degree;

- ideally, further clinical qualifications;
- at least 3 years' experience of microbiology;
- analytical skills;
- research skills;
- good communication skills.

# 10. PHARMACIST

## Main purpose of job

To provide full dispensary services, ensuring that medicines and drugs are correctly dispensed and that all dispensary procedures, guidelines, legal and medical requirements are followed.

## Main responsibilities

1. Dispense drugs and medicines as required in accordance with agreed procedures and guidelines.
2. Develop and implement all necessary procedures and guidelines to ensure the effective dispensing and control of drugs and medicines and monitor these to ensure that they are kept up to date.
3. Give professional pharmaceutical advice to medical and professional staff and customers.
4. Maintain all required records relating to the issues of drugs and medicines and ensure that these are kept confidential.
5. Take all necessary steps to ensure that drugs and medicines are stored securely and in the right conditions.
6. Develop and maintain all necessary procedures and controls to ensure that statutory requirements are complied with.
7. Maintain up-to-date knowledge of drugs and medicines and pharmacy practice to ensure that services provided are of the highest standard.
8. Observe all requirements to maintain a safe and healthy working environment.

## Knowledge, skills and experience required

The job requires:

● a degree in pharmacy;
● membership of the Royal Pharmaceutical Society;
● ideally, further clinical qualifications;
● at least 3 years' experience of working in a pharmacy;

- experience of drug monitoring;
- good interpersonal skills and experience of patient counselling;
- good communication skills.

# 11. PRODUCT DEVELOPMENT MANAGER

## Main purpose of job

To organize research into the development of new products to ensure the continuing growth and profitability of the company.

## Main responsibilities

1. Direct and control staff to ensure that they are appropriately motivated and trained and carry out their responsibilities to the required standards.
2. Develop and implement policies and programmes to research into the development of new products and modifications to existing ones to achieve the company's business objectives.
3. Maintain an awareness of technical developments in the industry to ensure that the company has up-to-date and relevant information.
4. Commission or carry out research into new and existing product performance for both company and competitor products.
5. Maintain close links with other departments and internal clients to ensure that the appropriate products are developed to meet customer needs.
6. Develop and control the budget for the department to ensure that all financial and cost objectives are met and targets are achieved within overall cost constraints.
7. Provide advice to managers and employees on all matters related to new product development.
8. Establish and maintain contacts with customers and potential customers to develop an awareness of their product requirements.

## Knowledge, skills and experience required

The job requires:

- a degree in a science or engineering subject;
- preferably an additional higher qualification achieved through research;
- at least 5 years' product development experience;

- thorough knowledge of the company's products;
- managerial experience;
- excellent interpersonal skills;
- problem-solving skills;
- creativity.

# 12. R&D DIRECTOR

## Main purpose of job

To direct and control the company's research and development function and commission research projects to ensure that the company is at the forefront of industry developments and continually improves products and services.

## Main responsibilities

1.  Direct and control the staff of the R&D department to ensure that they carry out their responsibilities effectively and that there is a safe and healthy work environment.
2.  Contribute to the development of the company's corporate strategy.
3.  Direct and control research projects to ensure that they deliver timely and cost-effective results which enhance the effectiveness of the company and its products.
4.  Develop and maintain contacts with relevant organizations in the industry for the exchange of ideas and information.
5.  Provide scientific guidance and advice to the Board to enable them to decide priorities and make cost-effective decisions.
6.  Commission research as necessary and monitor contract performance.
7.  Evaluate the most effective means of communicating R&D information and deliver this information using the identified approach.
8.  Contribute to the development of a research and development strategy for the organization.
9.  Control and monitor the R&D budget to ensure that money is spent effectively and within prescribed limits.
10. Investigate various sources of funding and opportunities for collaboration to ensure the most effective service to the company.

# Knowledge, skills and experience required

The job requires:

- higher degree in a scientific or research discipline;
- management experience of at least 10 years, including experience of managing a research team;
- a thorough understanding of the R&D environment;
- broad experience of the industry;
- an understanding of financial management and wider management principles and techniques;
- a high level of interpersonal skills.

## 13. RESEARCH MANAGER

## Main purpose of job

To lead and coordinate the research, analysis and coordination of information relevant to the development of the organization's strategy and policies and to provide a source of expertise to the organization.

## Main responsibilities

1.  Supervise a team of research and support staff, ensuring that they are appropriately trained and motivated and carry out their responsibilities to the required standards.
2.  Develop and implement research methods and work processes to ensure that a high standard of service is provided to the organization.
3.  Assist in the development of the organization's research policies to ensure that these support the overall mission and objectives.
4.  Develop and implement research programmes relevant to the organization and ensure that results are communicated clearly, concisely and accurately to managers and staff.
5.  Maintain and develop a comprehensive and up-to-date knowledge of research methods and developments to ensure that any research carried out is based on the best and most up-to-date methods and information.
6.  Review all research reports and publications to ensure a high degree of accuracy, clarity and readability.
7.  Develop and maintain contacts with external sources to ensure that the best possible information is gained and to provide effective advice to managers and staff.
8.  Represent the organization at external meetings and conferences on research issues, ensuring that a positive image of the organization is promoted.
9.  Oversee the research budget, ensuring that any research projects undertaken are relevant, accurately costed and provide value for money.

## Knowledge, skills and experience required

The job requires:

- higher degree in a scientific or research discipline;
- management experience of at least 5 years, including experience of managing a research team;
- a thorough understanding of the R&D environment;
- broad experience of the industry;
- an understanding of financial management and wider management principles and techniques;
- a high level of interpersonal skills.

## 14. RESEARCHER

## Main purpose of job

To carry out research and analysis and provide a source of expertise and advice on the interpretation and communication of economic, financial, statistical and scientific data to support the development of strategy and policies.

## Main responsibilities

1.  Design and implement surveys to collect data for use in business planning.
2.  Analyse data and prepare reports to communicate results accurately and clearly to managers and employees to assist in effective policy development and decision making.
3.  Develop and maintain databases for use by the organization and its employees.
4.  Maintain and develop a comprehensive and up-to-date knowledge of research techniques and developments to ensure that any analysis carried out is based on the best and most up-to-date information and methods.
5.  Develop and maintain contacts with external sources to ensure that the best possible information is gained and to provide effective advice to managers and staff.
6.  Represent the organization at external meetings and conferences on research issues, ensuring that a positive image of the organization is promoted.
7.  Maintain a comprehensive database of relevant research data.
8.  Respond to enquiries from managers and relevant external bodies relating to economic, financial, statistical and scientific data in the organization and the sector.
9.  Produce regular publications and use a variety of communications to ensure that managers and staff are kept up to date with research findings relevant to their jobs.

## Knowledge, skills and experience required

The job requires:

- a good degree in a relevant subject;
- at least 3 years' experience in research;
- thorough knowledge of the sector;
- thorough knowledge of company products and services;
- research and analysis skills;
- excellent numeracy;
- good interpersonal skills.

## 15. SENIOR ECONOMIST

# Main purpose of job

To lead a team carrying out economic research and analysis and provide a source of economic expertise and advice to support the development of strategy and policies.

# Main responsibilities

1.  Supervise a team of economists and support staff, ensuring that they are appropriately trained and motivated and carry out their responsibilities to the required standards.
2.  Develop and implement economic research methods and work processes to ensure that a high standard of service is provided to the organization.
3.  Assist in the development of the organization's economic policies to ensure that these support the overall mission and objectives.
4.  Carry out economic research and analysis in identified markets and communicate results to managers to assist in effective policy development and decision making.
5.  Maintain and develop a comprehensive and up-to-date knowledge of economic developments in the sector to ensure that any analysis carried out is based on the best and most up-to-date information.
6.  Respond to enquiries from managers and relevant external bodies relating to economic developments in the organization and the sector.
7.  Produce regular publications and use a variety of communications to ensure that managers and staff are kept up to date with economic developments relevant to their jobs.
8.  Develop and maintain contacts with external sources to ensure that the best possible information is gained and to provide effective advice to managers and staff.
9.  Represent the organization at external meetings and conferences on economic issues, ensuring that a positive image of the organization is promoted.
10. Maintain a comprehensive database of relevant economic information.

## Knowledge, skills and experience required

The job requires:

- a good economics degree;
- ideally a higher degree in economics or a related subject;
- at least 5 years' experience in economic analysis and research;
- experience of leading a professional team;
- thorough knowledge of the sector;
- thorough knowledge of company products and services;
- research and analysis skills;
- good interpersonal skills.

# 16. STATISTICIAN

## Main purpose of job

To carry out statistical research and analysis and provide a source of expertise and advice on the interpretation and communication of statistical data to support the development of strategy and policies.

## Main responsibilities

1. Design and implement surveys to collect statistical data for use in business planning.
2. Analyse statistical data and prepare reports to communicate results accurately and clearly to managers and employees.
3. Develop and maintain a statistical database for use by the organization and its employees.
4. Maintain and develop a comprehensive and up-to-date knowledge of statistical techniques and developments to ensure that any analysis carried out is based on the best and most up-to-date information and methods.
5. Develop and maintain contacts with external sources to ensure that the best possible information is gained and to provide effective advice to managers and staff.
6. Represent the organization at external meetings and conferences on statistical issues, ensuring that a positive image of the organization is promoted.
7. Maintain a comprehensive database of relevant economic information.
8. Respond to enquiries from managers and relevant external bodies relating to statistical data in the organization and the sector.

## Knowledge, skills and experience required

The job requires:

- a good degree in a relevant subject;
- at least 3 years' experience in statistical analysis;
- thorough knowledge of the sector;
- thorough knowledge of company products and services;

- research and analysis skills;
- excellent numeracy;
- good interpersonal skills.

# 13

# Sales and marketing

This section includes job descriptions for the following jobs:

1. Account manager
2. Area sales manager
3. Brand manager
4. Business development manager
5. Call centre supervisor
6. Commercial director
7. Credit manager
8. Customer relations manager
9. Customer services director
10. Director of marketing
11. Estimator
12. Market researcher
13. Marketing communications manager
14. National accounts manager
15. Product marketing manager
16. Sales administrator
17. Sales director
18. Sales executive
19. Technical sales manager

# 1. ACCOUNT MANAGER

## Main purpose of job

To generate sales from a portfolio of accounts in accordance with agreed targets and to maximize company profitability.

## Main responsibilities

1. Generate sales for a portfolio of accounts to achieve annual sales targets.
2. Research new sales opportunities within the existing portfolio of accounts and identify new potential customers within the allocated sales area.
3. Monitor feedback from customers to measure their satisfaction with company products.
4. Provide customers and potential customers within the allocated sales area with information about company products and services.
5. Maintain an awareness of sales and other developments amongst competitors and pass any relevant information to the appropriate company staff.
6. Maintain all required records of sales and other relevant information to enable performance to be measured and monitored.
7. Maintain an awareness of developments in sales generation and product development.

## Knowledge, skills and experience required

The job requires:

- a degree-level qualification;
- at least 2 years' experience of sales and marketing;
- thorough product knowledge;
- excellent communication and sales skills;
- a proven sales record.

## 2. AREA SALES MANAGER

## Main purpose of job

To direct and control the sales force for a geographical area within the company to achieve agreed sales volumes.

## Main responsibilities

1.  Organize and control area sales staff to ensure that they are appropriately motivated and trained to meet all sales targets and that they carry out their responsibilities to the required standards.
2.  Develop all necessary procedures and processes to ensure that the sales force operates efficiently and effectively and achieves all sales objectives.
3.  Monitor the performance of sales staff and take remedial action where necessary to ensure that sales targets are met.
4.  Monitor and control the budget for the area to ensure that all financial targets are met and that all necessary financial controls are in place to comply with company and regulatory requirements.
5.  Develop and maintain relationships with key customers and other relevant bodies to ensure that the company's maximum sales potential is realized in the area.
6.  Maintain an awareness of developments in sales techniques and technology to ensure that the company maintains and develops its competitive position.
7.  Monitor the sales performance of competitors to ensure that the company maintains and develops its competitive position.

## Knowledge, skills and experience required

The job requires:

- qualification to degree level;
- at least 5 years' sales management experience;
- thorough knowledge and experience of marketing and sales;
- thorough knowledge of company products;
- excellent sales and interpersonal skills;
- excellent planning and organizing skills;
- impressive record of achieving targets.

# 3. BRAND MANAGER

## Main purpose of job

To plan and organize the implementation of a brand strategy to ensure the development and protection of the brand.

## Main responsibilities

1. Plan and organize the implementation of the brand strategy to ensure the achievement of all targets in support of the brand strategy.
2. Direct and control staff in the implementation of branding activities and initiatives to ensure that they are appropriately motivated and trained and carry out their responsibilities to the required standards.
3. Evaluate customer research, market conditions and competitor data to implement brand-planning changes as needed.
4. Assist in the development of long-term brand strategy and implement short- to medium-term objectives in support of the strategy.
5. Provide support to product marketing to develop customer propositions and marketing communications.
6. Maintain regular contact with other functions and managers and particularly with legal advisers to ensure strong brand protection.
7. Provide the main source of expertise to the company in relation to brand development and maintain an awareness of any relevant developments in this field.

## Knowledge, skills and experience required

The job requires:

- education to degree level;
- ideally a relevant professional qualification;
- at least 5 years' brand management experience;
- excellent objective-setting and analytical skills;
- managerial skills;
- excellent communication and presentation skills;
- excellent interpersonal skills;

- ability to steer a complex organization towards consistent brand communications;
- computer skills.

# 4. BUSINESS DEVELOPMENT MANAGER

## Main purpose of job

To identify and develop new business opportunities which will help the company achieve its strategic and business objectives.

## Main responsibilities

1. Develop and implement information systems which will provide data on existing and potential customers to enable the company to identify opportunities for new sales.
2. Develop and implement systems and processes to enable the effective monitoring of performance and the identification of improvements in product quality and service delivery.
3. Carry out or commission surveys of customer satisfaction to identify the scope for improvements in product quality and service delivery.
4. Carry out or commission research in the company's existing and potential markets to identify new opportunities.
5. Assist other departments in the risk assessment of new products and services.
6. Assist in the development of sales and marketing literature and associated documents to improve the marketing of the company and its products.
7. Provide the main source of expertise to the company on business development issues.
8. Maintain regular contact with the sales and production functions to keep abreast of any developments in products and services.
9. Maintain an awareness of developments in the fields of product marketing and research to ensure that the company continues to compete effectively.

## Knowledge, skills and experience required

The job requires:

- education to degree level or equivalent;
- at least 5 years' experience in marketing and market research;

- thorough knowledge of company products and services;
- research and analysis skills;
- good interpersonal skills.

# 5. CALL CENTRE SUPERVISOR

## Main purpose of job

To supervise the staff of the call centre to ensure that they respond to all incoming calls to established standards and meet their performance targets.

## Main responsibilities

1. Supervise call centre staff to ensure that they are appropriately motivated and trained and carry out their responsibilities to the required standards.
2. Allocate workload to call centre staff, ensuring that it is evenly distributed and that business targets are met.
3. Monitor the service levels provided by the call centre to ensure that all quality standards are met.
4. Assist in the recruitment and selection of staff for the centre.
5. Maintain all required records of activity levels for management control purposes.
6. Investigate and resolve any problems arising in the course of providing the service.

## Knowledge, skills and experience required

The job requires:

- education to A-level standard;
- at least 3 years' experience of call centre operations;
- excellent supervisory skills;
- excellent interpersonal skills;
- commercial awareness;
- problem-solving skills;
- ability to use standard office software;
- excellent telephone manner.

## 6. COMMERCIAL DIRECTOR

## Main purpose of job

To develop and direct the implementation of commercial policies to improve current business and identify new market opportunities, and to ensure the effective development and promotion of the company's services and achievement of its business objectives.

## Main responsibilities

1. Identify and develop new initiatives to improve the range and quality of the services provided by the company and to ensure responsiveness to changes in the external environment.
2. Develop and implement all necessary commercial policies and procedures to ensure the effective promotion and marketing of the company and to meet business objectives.
3. Oversee research into new and established markets to develop products and services that meet market demands and which are consistent with the company's corporate strategy.
4. Develop and maintain effective communications with new and existing customers to negotiate contracts that contribute to corporate objectives.
5. Develop and maintain effective communications with internal managers to keep aware of the company's delivery capabilities and to inform them of new sales developments.
6. Promote and represent the interests of the company at senior levels, including to central and local government, key customers, the voluntary sector and commercial and trade organizations.
7. Direct and control the directorate's finances to ensure that all financial targets are met and to promote effective budgeting and cost control.
8. Contribute to the development of the company's corporate strategy, as part of the corporate management team, with particular reference to the development of the company's commercial objectives.
9. Direct and control the staff of the directorate to ensure that they are appropriately motivated and trained and are working towards the achievement of the company's corporate objectives.

## Knowledge, skills and experience required

The job requires:

- a degree-level qualification;
- at least 10 years' experience in the marketing function;
- extensive management experience;
- an established track record in the field of marketing;
- detailed knowledge of the company and its products;
- experience in the industry;
- interpersonal skills of the highest order.

# 7. CREDIT MANAGER

## Main purpose of job

To ensure that the objectives of the company's credit management policies are achieved.

## Main responsibilities

1. Develop and implement all necessary procedures and guidelines to ensure that the company's credit policy is effectively followed.
2. Monitor customer accounts to ensure that they do not exceed assigned credit limits.
3. Monitor all payments made to ensure that customers pay invoices in accordance with the agreed terms of sale.
4. Prepare reports on the credit standing of customers and advise the appropriate managers on commercial and financial risks and appropriate credit limits.
5. Gather and maintain up-to-date financial information on customers from various sources to determine an appropriate credit limit.
6. Maintain regular contact with customers so that any major change in credit status can be reported to the appropriate manager for action.
7. Arrange and negotiate the most appropriate and cost-effective form of credit insurance for the company.
8. Maintain an awareness of developments in the field of credit management so that the company maintains up-to-date policies and continues to comply with relevant regulations.

## Knowledge, skills and experience required

The job requires:

- a minimum of 5 years' experience of credit management;
- membership of an appropriate professional body;
- excellent communication and negotiation skills;
- an ability to work independently without close supervision.

## 8. CUSTOMER RELATIONS MANAGER

## Main purpose of job

To provide comprehensive support to customers in the use of company products and to respond to any difficulties encountered by them.

## Main responsibilities

1.  Provide training and support to customers in the use of company products so that they derive the maximum benefit from these.
2.  Provide training in company products to company staff and retailers to increase their sales effectiveness.
3.  Oversee the provision of help desk support to customers experiencing difficulties with company products.
4.  Pass any customer comments on products to research and development staff to enable them to identify any potential improvements in products.
5.  Attend exhibitions to demonstrate company products.
6.  Attend product launches to provide information and support in relation to those products.
7.  Conduct presentations to existing and potential customers in support of the sales and marketing functions.
8.  Recommend to sales and marketing and research and development staff any identified market needs for new or enhanced products.

## Knowledge, skills and experience required

The job requires:

- a degree or equivalent professional qualification;
- sales and marketing experience;
- training experience;
- excellent presentation and communication skills;
- good computer skills;
- technical knowledge about the company's products.

# 9. CUSTOMER SERVICES DIRECTOR

## Main purpose of job

To direct and control the Customer Services Department to ensure delivery of products and services which meet customers' requirements and achieve business targets in accordance with the company's corporate strategy.

## Main responsibilities

1. Direct and control the staff of the department to ensure that they are appropriately motivated and trained and carry out their responsibilities to the required standards.
2. Develop and implement a customer service strategy which provides total customer satisfaction and meets corporate objectives.
3. Develop and implement the department's budget to ensure that all business objectives are attained.
4. Oversee the department's finances to ensure that all revenue, profit and cost targets are met.
5. Develop and implement all necessary processes and procedures to ensure the achievement of high productivity with world-class quality processes and continuous improvement.
6. Identify and implement new working processes to improve the efficiency, effectiveness and quality of products and services.
7. Research and identify new business opportunities to ensure sustained growth.
8. Develop and maintain effective working relationships with key customers to develop more business opportunities.
9. Negotiate major contracts for the company to maximize profit margins.

## Knowledge, skills and experience required

The job requires:

- a degree-level qualification;
- at least 10 years' experience in the marketing or sales functions;
- extensive management experience;

- an established track record in the field of customer relations;
- detailed knowledge of the company and its products;
- experience in the industry;
- interpersonal skills of the highest order.

## 10. DIRECTOR OF MARKETING

## Main purpose of job

To develop and introduce marketing strategies to improve current business, identify new market opportunities and ensure the effective development and promotion of the company and its products.

## Main responsibilities

1. Identify and develop new initiatives to improve the range and quality of the products provided by the company and to ensure responsiveness to changes in the external environment.
2. Develop all necessary policies and procedures to ensure the effective promotion and marketing of the company.
3. Analyse trends in the business environment, help to develop products that are responsive to market demands, and identify new market opportunities.
4. Assist in formulating and monitoring the annual business plan to ensure the long-term success and viability of the company and the attainment of corporate objectives.
5. Critically evaluate the costs and benefits of all new ideas and initiatives to ensure that resources are appropriately directed and to keep the company ahead of its competitors.
6. Direct and control the staff of the directorate to ensure that they are appropriately motivated and trained and are working towards the achievement of the company's corporate objectives.
7. Advise the company, as part of the corporate management team, on the development of new initiatives and the promotion and marketing of products to ensure the achievement of the company's business plan and corporate objectives.
8. Control and monitor the directorate's finances to ensure effective budgeting and cost control.

## Knowledge, skills and experience required

The job requires:

- a degree-level qualification;

- at least 10 years' experience in the marketing function;
- extensive management experience;
- an established track record in the field of marketing;
- detailed knowledge of the company and its products;
- experience in the industry;
- interpersonal skills of the highest order.

# 11. ESTIMATOR

## Main purpose of job

To prepare quotations for the supply of company products following an on-site survey.

## Main responsibilities

1. Visit potential customers and carry out site surveys to enable quotations to be prepared for the supply of company products.
2. Prepare quotations following the site survey to agreed deadlines and standards.
3. Oversee subcontractors when quotes are required from them to carry out any necessary work.
4. Monitor the quality of quotations to ensure that they are accurate.
5. Keep customers and sales staff informed of any potential problems or likely delays to the completion of quotations.
6. Maintain all necessary records of quotations prepared and issued.

## Knowledge, skills and experience required

The job requires:

- education to GCSE level;
- at least 1 year's experience in technical estimating;
- thorough knowledge of company products;
- accuracy;
- good interpersonal skills.

# 12. MARKET RESEARCHER

## Main purpose of job

To research and analyse internal and external market information to enable the company to identify opportunities and develop products and services which will support business objectives.

## Main responsibilities

1. Develop and implement a market research policy that will enable the company to identify sales opportunities.
2. Carry out research, analyse results and produce reports identifying relevant market trends and recommending appropriate policies and actions to be implemented by the company.
3. Monitor research results to ensure that the policies and procedures adopted meet the company's requirements.
4. Support the production, sales and marketing functions, by providing them with research results which will assist in decision making.
5. Provide a source of expertise to managers and staff in carrying out market research.
6. Maintain an awareness of developments in the field of market research to ensure that the company continues to apply the most effective policies and approaches.

## Knowledge, skills and experience required

The job requires:

- education to degree level or equivalent;
- at least 3 years' experience in a marketing role;
- knowledge and experience of carrying out research and analysing results;
- numeracy and IT skills;
- thorough knowledge of the company and its products;
- excellent interpersonal skills;
- excellent presentation skills.

# 13. MARKETING COMMUNICATIONS MANAGER

## Main purpose of job

To develop and oversee all marketing promotions for the company's products.

## Main responsibilities

1. Develop plans for the advertising and marketing of company products to raise the company's market profile and increase sales.
2. Oversee the organization of promotional activities, ensuring that they are carried out efficiently and within agreed budgets, to raise the profile of the company and increase sales.
3. Coordinate all marketing plans and activities with other managers and staff in the company to ensure that the plans are delivered effectively.
4. Develop and control the company budget for marketing promotions.
5. Respond to internal and external requests for the development and provision of promotional activities.
6. Develop and maintain a stock of promotional material for issue to company staff and customers.
7. Arrange visits and hospitality for customers and others to promote the image of the company and its products.

## Knowledge, skills and experience required

The job requires:

- a degree-level qualification;
- at least 2 years' marketing experience;
- thorough knowledge of company products;
- excellent planning and organizational skills;
- excellent interpersonal and communication skills.

## 14. NATIONAL ACCOUNTS MANAGER

## Main purpose of job

To develop and implement sales policies and business plans for national accounts to meet agreed sales targets and key business objectives.

## Main responsibilities

1. Develop and implement sales policies and business plans for national accounts to meet agreed sales targets and business objectives.
2. Prepare and implement promotional and marketing plans for key accounts in consultation with other managers to meet business objectives.
3. Develop and maintain key contacts in national accounts to ensure the maintenance of good long-term relationships and to maximize sales of company products.
4. Monitor the progress towards the achievement of short- and long-term sales and business objectives and take any necessary action to ensure that these are achieved.
5. Maintain effective internal communication to ensure that all relevant company functions are kept informed of sales objectives and developments, particularly in relation to national accounts.
6. Monitor competitor activity in relation to national accounts and ensure that the appropriate responses are developed to any perceived threats to business.
7. Identify potential new accounts and take any required action to win these.

## Knowledge, skills and experience required

The job requires:

- a degree-level qualification;
- at least 5 years' account management experience;
- thorough knowledge of company products;
- excellent planning and organizational skills;
- excellent interpersonal and communication skills.

# 15. PRODUCT MARKETING MANAGER

## Main purpose of job

To direct and control the product marketing department to ensure that products are developed and delivered to meet identified customer needs.

## Main responsibilities

1. Direct and control the staff of the product marketing department to ensure that they are appropriately motivated and trained and carry out their responsibilities to the required standards.
2. Commission and carry out research to determine customer requirements for company products.
3. Commission and carry out research into all new product developments by competitors.
4. Identify any new developments required in existing products to maintain their competitiveness in the market.
5. Oversee research into new product developments to ensure that any required changes are made within the agreed timescale and budget.
6. Develop plans for the launch of new products into all relevant markets.
7. Monitor the product development budget to ensure that all targets are met within specified budget limits.
8. Maintain an awareness of new developments in the product development field to ensure that the company maintains its competitive advantage.

## Knowledge, skills and experience required

The job requires:

- a degree or relevant professional qualification;
- at least 5 years' experience in product development;
- a thorough understanding of the company and its markets;
- considerable sales and marketing experience;
- several years' management experience;
- highly developed interpersonal skills.

# 16. SALES ADMINISTRATOR

## Main purpose of job

To process orders from customers to ensure that they receive the right goods on the right date at the agreed price.

## Main responsibilities

1. Maintain regular contact with customers to identify their requirements.
2. Keep customers informed of the progress of their orders and ensure that they are notified of any possible delays.
3. Maintain customer stock levels to ensure that demand can be met within agreed notice periods.
4. Arrange stock deliveries to customers to ensure that the right goods are received on the right date.
5. Maintain accurate and up-to-date stock and delivery records.
6. Provide customers with information requested by them about stock and orders.
7. Maintain good relations with customers to ensure that the company remains as the preferred supplier.

## Knowledge, skills and experience required

The job requires:

- education to GCSE A level;
- at least 6 months' experience in sales administration;
- excellent telephone skills;
- good interpersonal skills;
- ability to maintain computerized records;
- good knowledge of the industry;
- thorough knowledge of the company's products;
- an awareness of ordering and distribution problems.

# 17. SALES DIRECTOR

## Main purpose of job

To direct and control the sales function for the company to achieve agreed sales volumes and develop policies and procedures that will meet the objectives of the company's sales strategy.

## Main responsibilities

1. Direct and control the company's sales staff to ensure that they are appropriately motivated and trained to meet all sales targets and that they carry out their responsibilities to the required standards.
2. Contribute to the development of the company's corporate strategy, particularly in relation to sales objectives.
3. Develop and implement sales strategies that enable the company to achieve its corporate objectives.
4. Develop all necessary procedures and processes to ensure that the sales function operates efficiently and effectively and achieves all sales objectives.
5. Monitor the performance of the sales function and take remedial action where necessary to ensure that sales targets are met.
6. Develop and control the budget for the sales function to ensure that all financial targets are met and that all necessary financial controls are in place to comply with company and regulatory requirements.
7. Develop and maintain relationships with key customers and other relevant bodies to ensure that the company's maximum sales potential is realized.
8. Maintain an awareness of developments in sales techniques and technology to ensure that the company maintains and develops its competitive position.
9. Monitor the sales performance of competitors to ensure that the company maintains and develops its competitive position.

## Knowledge, skills and experience required

The job requires:

- qualification to degree level;
- at least 10 years' sales management experience;
- thorough knowledge and experience of marketing and sales;
- thorough knowledge of company products;
- excellent sales and interpersonal skills;
- excellent planning and organizing skills;
- impressive record of achieving targets.

# 18. SALES EXECUTIVE

## Main purpose of job

To generate the maximum amount of profitable sales through the achievement of sales targets and by making new and existing customers aware of the company's product range.

## Main responsibilities

1.  Generate sales to achieve maximum profitability against annual sales targets.
2.  Identify and exploit new sales opportunities with existing and potential customers.
3.  Monitor customer accounts within the allocated sales area to ensure that sales potential is fully exploited.
4.  Establish and maintain effective communication links with other company departments to identify all sales opportunities.
5.  Maintain accurate records of all sales activity and prepare regular forecasts to enable effective forward planning.
6.  Maintain an awareness of company products and of relevant sales techniques to ensure that the sales role is carried out as effectively as possible.

## Knowledge, skills and experience required

The job requires:

- qualification to degree level;
- at least 1 year's proven sales experience;
- thorough knowledge of company products;
- excellent sales and interpersonal skills;
- good time management skills.

## 19. TECHNICAL SALES MANAGER

## Main purpose of job

To provide technical support to customers for all products supplied by the company so that they make the best use of those products and any problems are resolved.

## Main responsibilities

1. Maintain regular contact with customers to ensure that they are provided with all necessary technical support.
2. Respond to customer complaints and resolve any technical problems to ensure that company products are working effectively and the customer is satisfied with the service provided.
3. Provide feedback to any relevant company departments about complaints and problems to try to ensure that these do not arise in the future.
4. Investigate any claims made against the company by the customer and negotiate an acceptable settlement where possible.
5. Maintain an awareness of developments in products and in the industry in general and pass any relevant findings to the appropriate departments.
6. Organize site visits and product trials for prospective customers and report results to relevant managers in the company.
7. Maintain contact with the shipping department in relation to damage to goods, inspection of return loads etc.

## Knowledge, skills and experience required

The job requires:

- an appropriate technical qualification;
- at least 5 years' experience in the industry;
- detailed knowledge of products and processes;
- sales experience;
- excellent interpersonal and negotiating skills;
- knowledge of competitors' products, pricing and quality;
- good analytical and problem-solving skills.

# 14

# Secretarial and clerical

This section includes job descriptions for the following jobs:

1. Clerk/typist
2. Copy typist
3. Data input clerk/VDU operator
4. Filing clerk
5. Personal assistant/secretary to chief executive
6. Postal clerk
7. Receptionist
8. Receptionist and switchboard operator
9. Reprographics operator
10. Secretary
11. Telephone supervisor
12. Telephonist
13. Typing/word processing supervisor
14. Word processor operator

# 1. CLERK/TYPIST

## Main purpose of job

To provide clerical and typing support to a group of managers and staff.

## Main responsibilities

1. Type reports and correspondence from handwritten drafts, dictation or typed documents to laid-down standards and within specified time limits.
2. Sort documents from various sources into files alphabetically, by date or in any other prescribed order.
3. Collect, sort and distribute incoming and outgoing mail.
4. Photocopy, collate and distribute documents to managers and staff.
5. Maintain various internal records and produce reports summarizing data as required from time to time.
6. Assist with providing a reception service and in operating the telephone switchboard.
7. Attend and take notes at internal meetings.
8. Carry out other general clerical duties as required.

## Knowledge, skills and experience required

The job requires:

- education to GCSE level;
- typing skills at speed specified;
- good organizational skills;
- a high standard of English and knowledge of the rules of grammar;
- written presentation skills;
- ability to operate a range of office machinery.

## 2. COPY TYPIST

## Main purpose of job

To provide typing support to a group of managers and staff.

## Main responsibilities

1.  Type reports and correspondence from handwritten drafts, dictation or typed documents to laid-down standards and within specified time limits.
2.  Plan presentation and format of documents, including tables and graphics.
3.  Proof-read typed documents, making corrections where necessary.
4.  Organize work to meet priorities.
5.  Carry out other general clerical duties as required.

## Knowledge, skills and experience required

The job requires:

*   education to GCSE level;
*   typing skills at speed specified;
*   a high standard of English and knowledge of the rules of grammar;
*   written presentation skills;
*   ability to operate a word processor.

# 3. DATA INPUT CLERK/VDU OPERATOR

## Main purpose of job

To enter data by means of a computer terminal.

## Main responsibilities

1. Receive documents and enter relevant data into computer speedily and accurately via keyboard.
2. Review data to ensure that required information is provided.
3. Identify and report any data entry problems.

## Knowledge, skills and experience required

The job requires:

- a basic education only;
- keyboard skills;
- some work induction.

# 4. FILING CLERK

## Main purpose of job

To sort documents from various sources into files alphabetically, by date or in any other prescribed order.

## Main responsibilities

1. Sort documents according to prescribed criteria.
2. Classify material and place in file storage.
3. Locate and extract file information as requested.
4. Maintain a record of files borrowed.
5. Enter file data onto a computer and other storage media.
6. Remove old files to archives or other long-term storage in accordance with agreed procedures.
7. Maintain an indexing and cross-referencing system.

## Knowledge, skills and experience required

The job requires:

● a basic education only;
● some work induction.

# 5. PERSONAL ASSISTANT/SECRETARY TO CHIEF EXECUTIVE

## Main purpose of job

To provide a full secretarial and administrative support service to the chief executive.

## Main responsibilities

1. Provide a full secretarial and administrative support service to the chief executive.
2. Maintain the diary and arrange appointments as necessary.
3. Type reports and routine correspondence from dictation or written sources.
4. Screen and respond to all incoming telephone calls and take action as appropriate.
5. Draft routine correspondence for approval and signature by the chief executive.
6. Receive visitors to the office.
7. Open and distribute post.
8. Attend and minute all board meetings and arrange for the distribution of the minutes.
9. Maintain the office filing system and all personnel records.
10. Make all travel arrangements for the chief executive.
11. Make arrangements for any meetings required by the chief executive.
12. Undertake projects and research, which might require contact with external agencies, as required by the chief executive.
13. Operate standard office equipment such as word processor, photocopier etc.
14. Act as the chief executive's representative at internal meetings.
15. Oversee the maintenance of secretarial standards throughout the company and contribute to the training of other secretaries.

## Knowledge, skills and experience required

The job requires:

- education at least to A-level standard;
- at least 3 years' experience as a secretary;
- a full range of secretarial skills;
- excellent interpersonal skills;
- good organizing skills;
- tact and discretion.

## 6. POSTAL CLERK

## Main purpose of job

To collect and sort incoming and outgoing mail.

## Main responsibilities

1. Open and sort incoming mail and deliver to correct location.
2. Collect all outgoing mail from various locations.
3. Check and weigh outgoing mail to ensure that it is correctly addressed and franked or stamped.

## Knowledge, skills and experience required

The job requires:

- a basic education only;
- some work induction.

# 7. RECEPTIONIST

## Main purpose of job

To receive customers and visitors to the company and maintain the reception area to ensure that a good initial impression is given.

## Main responsibilities

1. Receive all visitors to the company, ensuring that their requirements are promptly dealt with and that they are given a favourable impression of the company.
2. Supervise the collection and delivery of incoming and outgoing mail to ensure that it is promptly delivered to the correct addresses, internally and externally.
3. Receive deliveries for staff in the building.
4. Issue and collect security passes and ensure visitors are entered into the visitors' book.
5. Reserve and allocate parking spaces to visitors.
6. Observe all necessary security arrangements.
7. Maintain the reception area in a tidy manner so that a favourable first impression is given to any visitors.
8. Maintain stocks of brochures, magazines and other information and ensure that these are easily accessible to visitors.

## Knowledge, skills and experience required

The job requires:

- smart appearance;
- an ability to communicate well verbally;
- good knowledge of the company and its staff.

# 8. RECEPTIONIST AND SWITCHBOARD OPERATOR

## Main purpose of job

To receive customers and visitors to the company and operate the telephone switchboard to ensure that a good initial impression is given and that the internal telephone communications system operates smoothly.

## Main responsibilities

1. Respond to all incoming telephone calls, ensuring that these are answered promptly and are directed to the right person in the company.
2. Receive all visitors to the company, ensuring that their requirements are promptly dealt with and that they are given a favourable impression of the company.
3. Supervise the collection and delivery of incoming and outgoing mail to ensure that it is promptly delivered to the correct addresses, internally and externally.
4. Maintain an up-to-date list of internal telephone numbers to ensure that incoming calls are directed to the right extension.
5. Receive deliveries for staff in the building.
6. Issue and collect security passes and ensure visitors are entered into the visitors' book.
7. Reserve and allocate parking spaces to visitors.
8. Observe all necessary security arrangements.
9. Maintain the reception area in a tidy manner so that a favourable first impression is given to visitors.

## Knowledge, skills and experience required

The job requires:

- an ability to operate the switchboard;
- a good telephone manner;
- smart appearance;
- an ability to communicate well verbally;
- good knowledge of the company and its staff.

# 9. REPROGRAPHICS OPERATOR

## Main purpose of job

To produce single or multiple copies of documents in various formats using photocopying and duplicating equipment.

## Main responsibilities

1.  Set up photocopying machine, making appropriate adjustments for size of paper, number of copies required and collation.
2.  Monitor production of copies to ensure that they are produced as required.
3.  Maintain stocks of paper and ink in the equipment used.
4.  Make any necessary minor adjustments to the equipment and take remedial action to correct problems such as paper jams, in accordance with manufacturer's handbook.
5.  Carry out routine cleaning and maintenance of the equipment.
6.  Report any malfunctions to relevant managers and arrange repairs and servicing.
7.  Maintain any required records of machine output.
8.  Place orders for new stocks of paper, toner, ink and other consumables as required.
9.  Bind or staple reports and documents in accordance with instructions and stack these for collection.

## Knowledge, skills and experience required

The job requires:

-   education to secondary school level;
-   knowledge of the photocopying equipment used;
-   knowledge of company standards in relation to reports;
-   ability to operate basic office equipment;
-   cooperative attitude.

# 10.  SECRETARY

## Main purpose of job

To provide full secretarial support service to an executive or group of executives.

## Main responsibilities

1.  Provide full secretarial and administrative support service to the executive.
2.  Maintain the diary and arrange appointments as necessary.
3.  Type reports and routine correspondence from dictation or written sources.
4.  Screen and respond to all incoming telephone calls and take action as appropriate.
5.  Draft routine correspondence for approval and signature by the executive.
6.  Receive visitors to the office.
7.  Open and distribute post.
8.  Maintain the office filing system and all personnel records.
9.  Make all travel arrangements for the executive.
10. Make arrangements for any meetings required by the executive.
11. Operate standard office equipment such as word processor, photocopier etc.

## Knowledge, skills and experience required

The job requires:

- education to A-level standard;
- at least 2 years' experience as a secretary;
- a full range of secretarial skills;
- excellent interpersonal skills;
- good organizing skills;
- tact and discretion.

# 11. TELEPHONE SUPERVISOR

## Main purpose of job

To supervise the operation of the company's telephone service to ensure that it provides a prompt, courteous and efficient response to callers.

## Main responsibilities

1. Supervise the company's telephonists to ensure that they are appropriately trained and carry out their responsibilities to the required standards.
2. Oversee the operation of the company's telephone service, ensuring that all calls are dealt with promptly, courteously and efficiently.
3. Organize a staffing rota to ensure that adequate cover is provided for the telephone service.
4. Maintain an answering machine service for out-of-hours callers, ensuring that the tape message is kept up to date.
5. Monitor feedback from users about suggested changes or improvements to the service to ensure that it continues to operate to high standards.
6. Oversee the maintenance and distribution of the internal telephone directory to ensure that users have up-to-date and accurate information.
7. Monitor the overall effectiveness of the telephone service and provide managers with reports on its operation and any changes required.
8. Report any faults with the service to relevant managers to ensure that action is taken to resolve problems.

## Knowledge, skills and experience required

The job requires:

- education to GCSE level;
- at least 2 years' experience as a telephonist;
- supervisory experience;
- excellent communication and interpersonal skills;
- good knowledge of the company and its staff.

# 12. TELEPHONIST

## Main purpose of job

To operate the telephone switchboard so that that a good initial impression is given and the internal communications system operates smoothly.

## Main responsibilities

1. Respond to all incoming telephone calls, ensuring that these are answered promptly and are directed to the right person in the company.
2. Place some outgoing calls, especially where the caller is having difficulty getting a connection.
3. Maintain an up-to-date list of internal telephone numbers to ensure that incoming calls are directed to the right extension.

## Knowledge, skills and experience required

The job requires:

- an ability to operate the switchboard;
- a good telephone manner;
- an ability to communicate well verbally;
- good knowledge of the company and its staff.

# 13. TYPING/WORD PROCESSING SUPERVISOR

## Main purpose of job

To supervise a team of word processor operators to produce typed reports, correspondence and other documentation to a high standard.

## Main responsibilities

1. Oversee the work of a group of word processor operators to ensure that they produce typed material to a consistently high standard.
2. Provide any necessary training and advice to staff to ensure that work is produced to the required standard.
3. Assist in the selection of new staff, including organizing the appropriate aptitude tests.
4. Oversee the maintenance of all machinery and equipment used and arrange emergency backup in the event of system failures, to ensure continuity of typing services.
5. Maintain all holiday and sickness records for staff of the section.
6. Type more complex or highly confidential reports and correspondence.

## Knowledge, skills and experience required

The job requires:

- education at least to GCSE level;
- an excellent standard of typing and presentation;
- at least 2 years' experience of working in a similar common services environment;
- supervisory experience;
- organizational skills;
- a high standard of English and knowledge of the rules of grammar.

## 14. WORD PROCESSOR OPERATOR

## Main purpose of job

To operate a word processor to produce reports and correspondence of a high standard and within required timescales.

## Main responsibilities

1. Produce reports and correspondence as required to laid-down standards and within specified time limits.
2. Decide most appropriate means of presentation and agree this with originator.
3. Type from handwritten drafts, dictation or typed documents and make any necessary changes to spelling, grammar and punctuation.
4. Notify the originator of any problems in meeting requirements.
5. Correct original drafts as required.

## Knowledge, skills and experience required

The job requires:

- education to GCSE level;
- typing skills at speed specified;
- good organizational skills;
- a high standard of English and knowledge of the rules of grammar;
- written presentation skills.

# 15

# Transport and distribution

This section includes job descriptions for the following jobs:

1.  Car fleet manager
2.  Depot manager
3.  Fleet engineer
4.  Garage manager
5.  Packing supervisor
6.  Supply chain manager
7.  Transport manager
8.  Warehouse manager
9.  Warehouseman

# 1. CAR FLEET MANAGER

## Main purpose of job

To oversee the company's policy relating to the provision of company cars to managers and staff.

## Main responsibilities

1.  Oversee the administration of the company's car policy to ensure that it is complied with in all respects.
2.  Advise managers and staff on all legal and compliance matters relating to vehicles.
3.  Maintain all necessary records to ensure that vehicles provided by the company comply with legal and business requirements.
4.  Maintain regular contact with the car leasing company and with vehicle manufacturers to ensure that the best deals are made for the company.
5.  Oversee car maintenance schedules to ensure that they are maintained in a safe and roadworthy condition.
6.  Maintain contact with relevant licensing authorities, the police and insurance companies on a range of issues relating to company cars.
7.  Maintain up-to-date knowledge of changes in legislation relating to cars and of the latest developments from manufacturers.

## Knowledge, skills and experience required

The job requires:

*   good secondary education;
*   at least 6 months' experience of the administration of company car policies;
*   knowledge of the motor industry and of vehicle manufacturers;
*   good communication skills.

# 2. DEPOT MANAGER

## Main purpose of job

To manage a transport depot, ensuring maximum profitability while maintaining the best possible standards of service and efficiency.

## Main responsibilities

1.  Direct and control all depot operations to ensure that profitability targets are achieved and that full utilization is made of both vehicles and staff while maintaining the highest standards of safety and efficiency.
2.  Maintain a close liaison with existing and potential customers to ensure that they are completely satisfied with the service provided.
3.  Develop any necessary procedures to ensure that vehicle maintenance, engineering and safety standards are strictly implemented and adhered to.
4.  Direct and control the staff of the depot to ensure that harmonious working relationships are maintained and to ensure that they are appropriately trained and motivated to carry out their responsibilities to the highest standards.
5.  Negotiate contracts with subcontractors to supplement the services provided by the company's own vehicles and monitor their performance to ensure that it meets the company's standards.
6.  Maintain regular contact with other depot managers to ensure the most effective utilization of vehicles across the company.

## Knowledge, skills and experience required

The job requires:

- a certificate of professional competence (CPC);
- at least 2 years' experience of transport management;
- complete understanding of transport industry legislation;
- knowledge of vehicle scheduling and planning;
- management experience;
- good communication skills.

# 3. FLEET ENGINEER

## Main purpose of job

To negotiate and maintain company-wide contracts for the purchase of equipment and supplies and to provide technical advice and support to the company and its managers in relation to transport engineering.

## Main responsibilities

1. Supervise garage and engineering staff to ensure that they are appropriately motivated and trained and carry out their responsibilities to the required standards.
2. Negotiate and maintain comprehensive company-wide contracts for the purchase of tyres, fuel, vehicles etc to ensure that the company is provided with the most cost-effective arrangements to meet identified requirements.
3. Oversee the management of contracts and provide advice on these to the company to ensure that effective relationships are maintained with suppliers and that contractual commitments are met.
4. Provide technical and engineering advice to managers and staff to ensure that vehicles and products purchased meet the company's business requirements and quality specifications.
5. Design and implement improvements to vehicles, trailers and other vehicles and equipment to ensure that these operate to maximum effectiveness and meet all required specifications.
6. Interpret and provide advice on transport legislation to ensure that the company complies with all legal requirements.
7. Devise and implement systems and procedures to ensure that the company complies with legal requirements.
8. Maintain all necessary records of vehicle operations to ensure that results can be analysed and performance improved where necessary.
9. Oversee the provision of a comprehensive vehicle maintenance service to the company's vehicle fleet.

# Knowledge, skills and experience required

The job requires:

- a relevant technical qualification;
- comprehensive technical knowledge of vehicles, traders and ancillary equipment;
- wide-ranging experience of the industry, probably gained over a period of at least 5 years;
- managerial experience;
- a thorough understanding of transport legislation;
- an ability to understand and apply computer technology to operations and records;
- excellent communication skills;
- excellent negotiation skills;
- excellent management skills.

# 4. GARAGE MANAGER

## Main purpose of job

To supervise a vehicle maintenance garage to ensure that the company's vehicles are effectively maintained and serviced.

## Main responsibilities

1.  Supervise staff in the garage to ensure that they are appropriately trained and motivated and carry out their responsibilities to the required standards.
2.  Oversee all vehicle maintenance operations to ensure that company vehicles are effectively maintained and serviced.
3.  Develop and implement maintenance service schedules to ensure that repairs and maintenance are carried out efficiently and at the appropriate times to minimize vehicle downtime.
4.  Negotiate contracts for vehicle maintenance as required and ensure that all contractual obligations are met to the required standards.
5.  Provide technical advice on vehicles, trailers and ancillary equipment to managers and staff to ensure that specifications are met and the company complies with legal requirements.
6.  Develop and monitor the operation of all necessary systems and procedures to ensure that vehicle and garage safety standards are adhered to.

## Knowledge, skills and experience required

The job requires:

- a relevant technical qualification;
- comprehensive technical knowledge of vehicles, traders and ancillary equipment;
- at least 3 years' experience of controlling a commercial garage;
- supervisory experience;
- an understanding of fleet management and transport legislation;
- good communication skills;
- good negotiation skills;
- good supervisory skills.

# 5. PACKING SUPERVISOR

## Main purpose of job

To supervise a team of packing operatives to ensure that they meet all packing targets to the specified quality standards.

## Main responsibilities

1. Supervise a team of operatives to ensure that they carry out their work effectively and safely.
2. Monitor the volume and quality of output to ensure that these are to the standards required.
3. Monitor machinery and adjust settings as necessary to ensure that the volume and quality of output are maintained to the required standard.
4. Receive and store raw materials to ensure that there are sufficient stocks to meet production requirements.
5. Monitor manning levels or make changes as necessary in the event of staff absence.
6. Address and resolve any technical issues arising in the packing process.
7. Train operators in the packing process to ensure that they work efficiently and safely.
8. Monitor the working environment to ensure that company and statutory hygiene and safety policies and regulations are complied with and to provide a safe and healthy working environment.
9. Maintain all necessary packing records.

## Knowledge, skills and experience required

The job requires:

- a technical qualification;
- through knowledge of the packaging process;
- thorough knowledge of the company and its products;
- supervisory skills and experience;
- good human relations skills.

# 6. SUPPLY CHAIN MANAGER

## Main purpose of job

To oversee the delivery, storage and despatch of all raw materials and finished products to ensure that the company meets all orders by the agreed dates.

## Main responsibilities

1. Supervise staff to ensure that they carry out their responsibilities to the required standards and receive all required training.
2. Oversee all goods in and ensure that these are unloaded and stored efficiently and safely.
3. Oversee the despatch operation to ensure that it operates efficiently, effectively and safely and meets customer requirements.
4. Oversee the use of the warehouse to ensure the maximum use of available space and a safe, efficient and profitable operation which meets customer and business needs.
5. Monitor all orders received and notify managers of production requirements to ensure that all production, despatch and delivery dates and targets are met.
6. Develop and implement effective stock control and audit systems to ensure that all stocks are maintained at the levels necessary to meet production requirements.
7. Oversee the use and maintenance of the company's vehicle fleet.
8. Negotiate contracts with hauliers to secure the most commercially favourable terms for the company.
9. Maintain regular contact with the production and packaging operations to ensure that there is effective coordination and that customer requirements are met.
10. Provide advice and guidance to company managers and staff on warehouse utilization, logistics, pallet control, transport costs etc.

## Knowledge, skills and experience required

The job requires:

- a relevant technical qualification;

- at least 5 years' experience of warehousing and logistics;
- managerial experience;
- good communication skills;
- good interpersonal skills;
- excellent organizational skills.

# 7. TRANSPORT MANAGER

## Main purpose of job

To direct and control the activities of transport depots to ensure the most cost-effective use of resources and to provide a high quality service to customers.

## Main responsibilities

1. Direct and control staff in transport depots to ensure that they carry out their responsibilities effectively and provide a high quality service to customers.
2. Assist in the development of the company's transport strategy to ensure the provision of the best possible quality of service and to maximize company profitability.
3. Develop and maintain the transport budget to ensure that services are provided to the required standard and within budgeted limits.
4. Develop an integrated network of transport services to ensure that the best possible use is made of company transport resources.
5. Maintain regular contact with customers to resolve any problems, identify new business opportunities and improve service levels and efficiency.
6. Maintain harmonious employment relations and ensure that all staff are appropriately trained and motivated.
7. Develop and maintain good relationships with outside agencies to ensure that the company complies with all legal requirements and regulations and to enhance the company's reputation.
8. Develop all necessary systems and procedures to ensure that the highest standards of engineering and safety are maintained and that all statutory requirements are met.
9. Provide advice to managers and staff on all transport related issues.
10. Maintain an awareness of new developments in transport to ensure that the company continues to provide the most effective service possible and complies with all regulations.

## Knowledge, skills and experience required

The job requires:

- a certificate of professional competence (CPC);
- qualifications to degree level or equivalent;
- at least 10 years' experience of managing a transport business;
- significant knowledge of transport legislation and road haulage;
- an ability to develop new business;
- excellent interpersonal skills;
- substantial management experience;
- excellent negotiating skills.

# 8. WAREHOUSE MANAGER

## Main purpose of job

To direct and control the use of warehouse facilities to ensure the maximum use of available space consistent with efficiency, safety and profitability.

## Main responsibilities

1. Direct and control the use of the warehouse to ensure the maximum use of available space and a safe, efficient and profitable operation which meets customer and business needs.
2. Pursue opportunities for new business to maximize the use of available warehouse space.
3. Oversee the despatch operation to ensure that it operates efficiently, effectively and safely and meets customer requirements.
4. Maintain a liaison with the production and transport operations to ensure that there is effective coordination of all operations and that customer requirements are met.
5. Provide advice and guidance to company managers and staff on warehouse utilization, logistics, pallet control, transport costs etc.
6. Carry out projects relating to the use of the warehouse and logistics to improve operational effectiveness.
7. Direct and control the staff of the warehouse to ensure that they are appropriately trained and motivated and carry out their responsibilities to the required standards.
8. Maintain all necessary records of goods stored and despatched.

## Knowledge, skills and experience required

The job requires:

- secondary education;
- at least 5 years' experience in the warehousing and distribution field;
- knowledge of distribution and logistics;
- knowledge of the industry;
- managerial experience;
- good negotiating skills;
- good communication skills.

# 9. WAREHOUSEMAN

## Main purpose of job

To assist in the loading, unloading and storage of finished goods and raw materials.

## Main responsibilities

1. Unload deliveries of raw materials from vans.
2. Store goods in appropriate section of warehouse as directed.
3. Drive forklift truck to load and unload goods.
4. Operate other plant, such as trolleys, to transport goods.
5. Monitor product quality and report any problems to manager.
6. Observe all health, safety and hygiene rules.

## Knowledge, skills and experience required

The job requires:

- secondary education;
- some experience in warehousing;
- ability to drive a forklift truck.

# 16

# Voluntary sector

This section includes job descriptions for the following jobs:

1. Company secretary (charity)
2. Donations administrator
3. Fundraiser
4. Fundraising assistant
5. Fundraising manager
6. Income clerk
7. Publications administrator
8. Publicity manager
9. Volunteer coordinator

# 1. COMPANY SECRETARY (CHARITY)

## Main purpose of job

To coordinate all arrangements for meetings of the Board of Trustees and committees to ensure that they are properly organized and conducted, and to implement all necessary policies and procedures to ensure that the organization complies with its statutory obligations.

## Main responsibilities

1. Coordinate all arrangements for meetings of the Board and management committees to ensure that they are properly organized and conducted and that minutes are accurately recorded and circulated.
2. Advise the Board and management committees on all statutory and constitutional requirements to ensure that business is conducted in a proper and effective manner.
3. Circulate decisions of the Board and committees to all relevant parties and take any necessary follow-up action to record progress on these.
4. Keep Board and committee members informed of all issues relevant to them and provide any necessary training and induction to ensure that they are aware of their responsibilities and of procedure.
5. Prepare any returns and records required by statute to ensure that the organization conducts its business in a legal and proper manner.
6. Prepare the annual report of the organization in accordance with legal and constitutional requirements.
7. Maintain the membership records of the Board and management committees.
8. Oversee the arrangements for the conduct of elections to the Board and committees.
9. Maintain all required legal records and act as custodian of key documents.

## Knowledge, skills and experience required

The job requires:

- a qualified company secretary or lawyer;
- at least 10 years' experience as a company secretary or lawyer;
- good knowledge of the organization;
- excellent organizational and time management skills;
- good interpersonal skills.

## 2. DONATIONS ADMINISTRATOR

## Main purpose of job

To record, acknowledge and maintain a record of all donations received.

## Main responsibilities

1.  Maintain a database of all appeals and of responses received.
2.  Acknowledge and maintain a record of all donations received.
3.  Respond to inquiries from donors and potential donors relating to donations.
4.  Send out literature and provide information relating to appeals.
5.  Maintain budgetary and cost records relating to appeals and donations.
6.  Recommend any necessary changes to, or developments of, information systems required to maintain records of donations and appeals.
7.  Maintain regular contact with internal staff on all matters relating to donations and appeals.

## Knowledge, skills and experience required

The job requires:

- qualification to A-level standard;
- at least one year's experience of administering and donations and appeals;
- good knowledge of the organization;
- organizational skills.

## 3. FUNDRAISER

## Main purpose of job

To implement policies to raise funds for the organization.

## Main responsibilities

1. Assist in the development of policies and procedures designed to maximize the funds received by the organization.
2. Apply fundraising policies and procedures to meet agreed income targets.
3. Develop and control appeals and other fundraising activities.
4. Develop and control a national organization of street collections to contribute to fund income.
5. Recruit and train fundraising volunteers.
6. Give presentations on the work of the organization to encourage fundraising and to promote the aims and objectives of the organization.
7. Maintain all necessary records of fund income and prepare reports as required.

## Knowledge, skills and experience required

The job requires:

- qualification to degree level;
- at least 2 years' experience in fundraising;
- good knowledge of the voluntary sector;
- excellent interpersonal skills.

## 4. FUNDRAISING ASSISTANT

## Main purpose of job

To provide administrative support to staff engaged in raising funds for the organization.

## Main responsibilities

1.  Maintain all administrative processes and records to support staff in carrying out fundraising activities for the organization.
2.  Apply fundraising policies and procedures to meet agreed income targets.
3.  Develop and control appeals and other fundraising activities.
4.  Develop and control a national organization of street collections.
5.  Recruit and train fundraising volunteers.
6.  Give presentations on the work of the organization to encourage fundraising and to promote the aims and objectives of the organization.
7.  Maintain all necessary records of fund income and prepare reports as required.

## Knowledge, skills and experience required

The job requires:

- qualification to degree level;
- at least 2 years' experience in fundraising;
- good knowledge of the voluntary sector;
- excellent interpersonal skills.

# 5. FUNDRAISING MANAGER

## Main purpose of job

To develop policies and processes to maximize the fund income for the organization.

## Main responsibilities

1. Develop and implement a national strategy to maximize the fund income to the organization.
2. Direct and control fundraising staff to ensure that they are appropriately motivated and trained and carry out their responsibilities to the required standards.
3. Develop fundraising targets and implement procedures to achieve those targets.
4. Develop a fundraising budget and take all necessary actions to achieve budget targets.
5. Research public and private sector organizations to maximize grant income and to identify potential donors.
6. Organize national and local fundraising appeals to increase the organization's income.
7. Recruit and train fundraising groups and individuals to increase the organization's income.
8. Raise and maintain awareness of the organization's activities to ensure maximum publicity and to encourage donations.
9. Develop and implement all necessary administrative procedures to ensure that the department functions effectively.

## Knowledge, skills and experience required

The job requires:

- qualification to degree level;
- at least 5 years' experience in fundraising;
- good knowledge of the voluntary sector;
- managerial experience;
- excellent interpersonal skills.

# 6. INCOME CLERK

## Main purpose of job

To ensure that all charitable income is correctly processed and accounted for.

## Main responsibilities

1. Maintain records of all covenants and gift aid, corresponding as necessary with donors.
2. Record legacies due, corresponding as necessary with solicitors, next of kin and any other relevant parties.
3. Oversee all bank accounts relating to income received and closely monitor cash balances and transfers from and into accounts.
4. Collect and record all income received from other sources.
5. Maintain a regular reconciliation between the income ledger and other ledgers.

## Knowledge, skills and experience required

The job requires:

- qualification to GCSE level;
- at least 1 year's experience in an accountancy function;
- knowledge of the voluntary sector;
- accuracy;
- honesty and integrity.

# 7. PUBLICATIONS ADMINISTRATOR

## Main purpose of job

To oversee the publication of all printed material sent out by the organization to ensure that it is in accordance with agreed standards and promotes the image of the organization.

## Main responsibilities

1. Draft detailed specifications and commission external suppliers for the design and printing of publications.
2. Monitor the production of all publications through all stages, ensuring that they are produced to the required standards and to agreed deadlines.
3. Coordinate copy, photographs, illustrations etc and provide support with copywriting.
4. Maintain all required records and check and authorize invoices for work carried out.
5. Order stationery as required and ensure that this is produced with the organization's corporate identity.
6. Proof-read all documents.
7. Monitor stock levels of publicity brochures and reorder printed material as required.
8. Maintain regular contact with all departments to ascertain their print requirements and place orders to meet these.
9. Coordinate the production and despatch of the organization's newsletter.

## Knowledge, skills and experience required

The job requires:

- qualification to degree level;
- good knowledge of the printing and production process;
- good knowledge of the voluntary sector;
- proof-reading skills;
- negotiating skills;
- good interpersonal skills.

# 8. PUBLICITY MANAGER

## Main purpose of job

To promote the public image of the organization through advertising, direct marketing and any other appropriate PR techniques.

## Main responsibilities

1. Develop policies and processes which directly contribute to the promotion of the organization's public image.
2. Direct and control public relations staff to ensure that they are appropriately motivated and trained and carry out their responsibilities to the required standards.
3. Develop and direct campaigns for the promotion of the organization's policies and to encourage fundraising.
4. Develop a media relations programme with appropriate print and broadcast media to raise awareness of the organization and its policies.
5. Develop and maintain effective contacts with a wide range of external bodies, including contractors and suppliers, to ensure wide publicity and cost-effective support for the organization's policies and activities.
6. Develop a range of publications to promote the organization and its policies.
7. Draft press releases and articles for publication to promote the image of the organization.
8. Negotiate contracts with suppliers for any services which cannot be provided in-house and monitor performance to ensure that they are of the standard required.
9. Develop and control the department's budget to ensure that services are provided within agreed financial limits.
10. Develop an internal communications network to ensure that all staff are kept informed of the organization's policies and achievements and to get source material for publicity purposes.
11. Provide the main source of expertise and advice to managers and staff on all matters with public relations implications.

12.  Keep abreast of developments within the field of public relations to ensure that the organization maintains the highest standards of public relations.

## Knowledge, skills and experience required

The job requires:

- qualification to degree level;
- at least 5 years' experience in public relations;
- good knowledge of the voluntary sector;
- managerial experience;
- excellent interpersonal skills.

## 9. VOLUNTEER COORDINATOR

## Main purpose of job

To recruit and train volunteers to assist with providing support to the charity and its clients.

## Main responsibilities

1. Establish the requirement for voluntary support by assessing the needs of clients and the support available from other sources.
2. Recruit and train volunteers to ensure that they are able to carry out the work required to the required standards.
3. Publicize the need for volunteers to ensure the best possible response.
4. Maintain all required records to ensure that the activities of volunteers are recorded and that expenses incurred are correctly reimbursed.
5. Provide support, advice and guidance to volunteers to ensure that they carry out their responsibilities effectively.
6. Provide any required stationery and equipment, ensuring that stocks are maintained at the appropriate levels.
7. Maintain all necessary budgetary and cost records to ensure that the costs of voluntary support are accurately recorded.
8. Maintain a regular liaison with internal staff to ensure that they are aware of the role and contribution of volunteers to the provision of the organization's services.

## Knowledge, skills and experience required

The job requires:

- qualification to degree level;
- at least 2 years' experience in the sector;
- organizational skills;
- managerial skills;
- excellent interpersonal skills.

# Part 2

# Job elements

# 17

# Providing advice and guidance

## ADMINISTRATION AND MANAGEMENT

- Provide advice to applicants and potential applicants about award and grant requirements and how to complete applications.
- Provide advice and guidance to managers and staff on all aspects of business transformation.
- Provide strategic advice and guidance to the chairman and the members of the Board, to keep them aware of developments within the industry and to ensure that the appropriate policies are developed to meet the company's mission and objectives and to comply with all relevant statutory and other regulations.
- Advise the chairman and committee members on correct committee procedure.
- Advise the Board and management committees on all statutory and constitutional requirements to ensure that business is conducted in a proper and effective manner.
- Advise managers and staff of the administrative support implications of operational changes.

- Provide support and advice to new and existing members to ensure that they gain the maximum benefit from membership of the association.

# ENGINEERING AND PRODUCTION

- Provide expert technical advice on all aspects of electrical engineering to other managers and staff to ensure effective decision making.
- Provide expert technical advice on all aspects of mechanical engineering to other managers and staff to ensure effective decision making.
- Advise on the purchase of plant and machinery to ensure that it is appropriate for the purposes intended.
- Provide technical advice and support to other departments.
- Provide expert advice and assistance on technical problems relating to the modification of products and equipment.
- Provide advice and support to other departments on production issues.
- Provide the main source of advice and guidance to the company and its managers on health and safety matters.
- Advise other maintenance personnel on any technical issues beyond their scope.
- Provide support and advice to other departments in the company to ensure that they are aware of their obligations in complying with environmental standards.
- Act as the company's main adviser on all issues relating to operational functions and keep abreast of latest developments to ensure that the company maintains its competitive position.
- Provide advice and guidance to managers and staff on the most efficient and effective engineering processes to meet production requirements.
- Provide advice on quality issues to managers and staff.
- Act as the company's expert on quality management and provide any necessary training and advice to managers and staff to ensure that they pursue the objectives of total quality management and continuous improvement.

- Provide advice and guidance to the company, its managers and staff on any regulatory aspects of total quality management.
- Provide advice and guidance to managers and staff on total quality management and continuous improvement.
- Provide any necessary training and advice to shift personnel to ensure that they carry out their responsibilities effectively.
- Advise on construction methods, materials, quality and safety standards to ensure that plant and equipment, working methods and processes comply with design specifications and identified standards.

## ESTATES AND SURVEYING

- Advise client on details of the proposed construction, including impact on surrounding area, and keep informed of progress.
- Advise managers and staff of the organization on all matters relating to building maintenance and modernization to ensure that properties are maintained to the required standards.
- Act as the company's principal adviser on matters relating to estates and surveying.
- Advise on financial and contractual issues relating to bills of quantities provided in relation to material supplied for construction projects.

## FINANCE AND ACCOUNTANCY

- Contribute to the achievement of the company's business objectives by providing advice and guidance on financial strategy.
- Provide financial advice and guidance to the company's managers and staff to enable them to achieve their objectives.
- Provide advice on financial accountancy issues to managers and staff as required.
- Give any necessary advice on management accountancy issues to ensure that managers and staff understand financial and budgetary requirements.
- Provide any required advice and guidance on payroll matters to managers and staff.

- Provide advice to staff and managers on matters related to pay, taxation and National Insurance.
- Provide advice and guidance to managers and staff on the interpretation and implementation of financial regulations and accountancy codes of practice.
- Provide information and assistance to managers and staff to enable them to comply with financial and statutory requirements.
- Provide advice to managers and staff on data obtained, highlighting any particular problem areas, so that any necessary remedial action can be taken.
- Act as the main budget contact for specific departments, assisting with the setting and monitoring of those budgets and providing all other advice and assistance those budget holders require.
- Provide information and advice on financial management, financial control and procedures, and information systems to the Board, directors and staff to ensure that the company's mission and financial and IS objectives are met.

## FINANCIAL SERVICES

- Advise clients or employer on the suitability of investments to ensure the best returns consistent with the investment policy.
- Advise the company on the suitability of investments to ensure the best returns consistent with the investment policy.
- Act as the company's principal adviser on all matters relating to taxation to ensure that the company's tax liabilities are optimized.
- Undertake any necessary research and provide expertise and advice on any matters of general concern and interest to the company in the underwriting and claims fields.
- Provide guidance and assistance to the sales force, including the preparation of suitable training and publicity material to ensure that they are able to provide a sound service.

## HUMAN RESOURCES/PERSONNEL

- Advise managers and staff on reward issues.

- Provide advice and guidance to managers and staff on all aspects of organization development and change.
- Advise managers on all aspects of employee relations and on the interpretation of joint agreements.
- Provide the main source of advice and guidance to the company and its managers on health and safety matters.
- Advise the organization on the staffing implications of new policies, products and services.
- Advise managers and staff of the organization on job evaluation and equal value issues.
- Advise the senior managers of the company about the personnel policies, procedures and actions required to ensure that the company makes the best use of its employees.
- Provide a comprehensive personnel advisory service to all company managers and staff to ensure that the company follows best practice in the management of its staff and to ensure compliance with legal requirements.
- Provide advice to line managers on best practice in all aspects of employment, including company policies and legislation.
- Provide an advisory service to all employees and employee representatives on company employment policies and procedures.
- Provide advice to managers on a range of employment issues to ensure that they manage their staff in accordance with best practice and legal requirements.
- Provide support and advice to managers on the planning of their workforce requirements.

## INFORMATION TECHNOLOGY

- Provide an organization-wide advisory and consultancy service on all aspects of data management.
- Provide a company-wide source of expertise on information technology and communications to ensure that managers and staff have the best possible information for effective decision making and accessing data.
- Provide a source of advice to managers and staff on information technology issues.

- Represent the department on project teams to ensure that the best possible advice is given about the implications of any new IT systems and proposed changes.
- Maintain an awareness of developments in the IT field and act as a source of advice and expertise to managers and staff within the company.
- Provide training and advice as required to users of information systems to ensure that they make the best use of those systems.
- Provide technical advice and guidance on programming matters to colleagues and system users.
- Act as the in-house expert on all software issues and provide advice and training to company management and staff as required.

# LEGAL

- Assist in providing accurate legal advice on less complex matters to managers and staff to ensure that decisions taken are legally correct.
- Provide accurate legal advice to managers and staff to ensure that decisions taken are legally correct and that the company's interests are protected.
- Provide legal advice to managers and staff on the interpretation of statutes and legal documents to ensure that the actions they take are legally sound.
- Provide accurate legal advice to managers and staff to ensure that decisions taken are legally correct.

# PUBLIC RELATIONS AND MEDIA

- Give strategic advice to the managers and staff in relation to their dealings with the media, to promote the public profile of the organization.
- Advise authors on the content and presentation of items for publication to ensure that they are of the required standard and are produced at the right time.
- Advise managers and staff on the design, presentation and cost-effectiveness of their print requirements.

- Provide technical advice on all aspects of the production process to company staff and external contractors so that they are fully aware of production requirements.
- Provide expertise and advice to managers and staff on all matters with public relations implications.
- Provide advice and support on public relations issues to managers and staff to ensure that a positive image of the organization is promoted.

## PURCHASING AND STORES

- Act as the company's adviser on all matters relating to the purchasing function.

## RESEARCH AND DEVELOPMENT (R&D) AND SCIENCE

- Provide the main source of expertise to the company on business development issues.
- Give professional pharmaceutical advice to medical and professional staff and customers.
- Develop and maintain contacts with external sources to ensure that the best possible information is gained and to provide effective advice to managers and staff.
- Determine and advise on suitable materials and processes to achieve sound and durable structures.
- Advise on specific geological problems and suggest solutions.
- Advise on the development of policies relating to antibiotics, use of disinfectants and infection control.
- Provide advice to managers and employees on all matters related to new product development
- Provide scientific guidance and advice to the Board to enable them to decide priorities and make cost-effective decisions.
- Develop and maintain contacts with external sources to ensure that the best possible information is gained and to provide effective advice to managers and staff.

# SALES AND MARKETING

- Provide customers and potential customers within the allocated sales area with information about company products and services.
- Provide the main source of expertise to the company on business development issues.
- Prepare reports on the credit standing of customers and advise the appropriate managers on commercial and financial risks and appropriate credit limits.
- Advise the company, as part of the corporate management team, on the development of new initiatives and the promotion and marketing of products to ensure the achievement of the company's business plan and corporate objectives.
- Provide a source of expertise to managers and staff on carrying out market research.

# TRANSPORT AND DISTRIBUTION

- Advise managers and staff on all legal and compliance matters relating to vehicles.
- Provide technical and engineering advice to managers and staff to ensure that vehicles and products purchased meet the company's business requirements and quality specifications.
- Interpret and provide advice on transport legislation to ensure that the company complies with all legal requirements.
- Provide technical advice on vehicles, trailers and ancillary equipment to managers and staff to ensure that specifications are met and the company complies with legal requirements.
- Provide advice and guidance to company managers and staff on warehouse utilization, logistics, pallet control, transport costs etc.
- Provide advice to managers and staff on all transport-related issues.

# VOLUNTARY SECTOR

- Advise the Board and management committees on all statutory and constitutional requirements to ensure that business is conducted in a proper and effective manner.

- Provide the main source of expertise and advice to managers and staff on all matters with public relations implications.
- Provide support, advice and guidance to volunteers to ensure that they carry out their responsibilities effectively.

# 18

# Customer/client relations

## ADMINISTRATION AND MANAGEMENT

- Maintain regular contact with customers to keep them aware of business developments and to seek feedback from them so that the company can effectively implement a programme of continuous improvement.
- Establish and maintain effective formal and informal links with major customers, relevant government departments and agencies, local authorities, key decision-makers and other stakeholders generally, to exchange information and views and to ensure that the company is providing the appropriate range and quality of services.
- Develop and maintain an effective marketing and public relations strategy to promote the products, services and image of the company in the wider community.
- Maintain regular contact with external agencies to promote the use of the association and its members.
- Represent the association at external events to promote the image of the association and to increase membership.

- Maintain an awareness of customer requirements and any complaints to identify any areas that may need development or improvement.

## ENGINEERING AND PRODUCTION

- Respond to any customer complaints to ensure that these are dealt with speedily and effectively.
- Develop and maintain good working relationships with customers and suppliers and organize periodic site visits to demonstrate the effectiveness of the production process.
- Maintain an awareness of customer requirements and any complaints to identify any areas that may need development or improvement.
- Give customers any necessary product information which might help them resolve minor problems and determine when a service visit is necessary.
- Make customers aware of any new product developments to increase company sales.
- Arrange visits for customers and prospective customers to company sites to develop and maintain their interest in company products and services.
- Negotiate with customers in the event of any claims against the company.
- Respond to technical inquiries from customers and ensure that any problems presented are resolved to their satisfaction.

## ESTATES AND SURVEYING

- Represent the function at external meetings with clients and potential clients to ensure that the services of the company are presented in the best light.

# FINANCE AND ACCOUNTANCY

- Respond to customer enquiries and complaints, by telephone or in writing, after having checked the relevant facts from existing records.
- Investigate any complaints by customers that might result in them disputing invoices or withholding payments.

# FINANCIAL SERVICES

- Promote the bank's image in the community by attendance at internal and external meetings and participation in community activities.
- Respond to occasional client queries to ensure that these are resolved effectively and sensitively.
- Provide an efficient and effective service to clients by maintaining effective communication with them, responding promptly to enquiries and negotiating contracts.

# INFORMATION TECHNOLOGY

- Represent the company as required at meetings with customers and external contractors to ensure that the software design implications of any proposals are thoroughly considered and to help maximize sales.

# LEGAL

- Represent the organization at meetings with external bodies to ensure that the legal aspects of any decisions are fully considered.

# LEISURE SERVICES

- Maintain a liaison with members of the public and all the users of the centre to ensure that they receive the best possible customer care.

# RESEARCH AND DEVELOPMENT (R&D) AND SCIENCE

- Establish and maintain contacts within the organization and with external customers to acquire information and to ensure that they are kept informed of relevant developments.
- Maintain a liaison with staff, customers and relevant external bodies to obtain information and report on research findings.
- Carry out or commission surveys of customer satisfaction to identify the scope for improvements in product quality and service delivery.
- Develop and maintain contacts with external sources to ensure that the best possible information is gained and to provide effective advice to managers and staff.
- Represent the organization at external meetings and conferences on economic issues, ensuring that a positive image of the organization is promoted.
- Establish and maintain contacts with customers and potential customers to develop an awareness of their product requirements.
- Develop and maintain contacts with external sources to ensure that the best possible information is gained and to provide effective advice to managers and staff.

# SALES AND MARKETING

- Monitor feedback from customers to measure their satisfaction with company products.
- Provide customers and potential customers within the allocated sales area with information about company products and services.
- Develop and maintain relationships with key customers and other relevant bodies to ensure that the company's maximum sales potential is realized in the area.
- Carry out or commission surveys of customer satisfaction to identify the scope for improvements in product quality and service delivery.
- Develop and maintain effective communications with new and existing customers to negotiate contracts that contribute to corporate objectives.

- Promote and represent the interests of the company at senior levels, including to central and local government, key customers, the voluntary sector and commercial and trade organizations.
- Maintain regular contact with customers so that any major change in credit status can be reported to the appropriate manager for action.
- Oversee the provision of help desk support to customers experiencing difficulties with company products.
- Conduct presentations to existing and potential customers in support of the sales and marketing functions.
- Develop and implement a customer service strategy which provides total customer satisfaction and meets corporate objectives.
- Develop and maintain effective working relationships with key customers to develop more business opportunities.
- Keep customers and sales staff informed of any potential problems or likely delays to the completion of quotations.
- Arrange visits and hospitality for customers and others to promote the image of the company and its products.
- Develop and maintain key contacts in national accounts to ensure the maintenance of good long-term relationships and to maximize sales of company products.
- Maintain regular contact with customers to identify their requirements.
- Keep customers informed of the progress of their orders and ensure that they are notified of any possible delays.
- Provide customers with information requested by them about stock and orders.
- Maintain good relations with customers to ensure that the company remains as the preferred supplier.
- Develop and maintain relationships with key customers and other relevant bodies to ensure that the company's maximum sales potential is realized.
- Maintain regular contact with customers to ensure that they are provided with all necessary technical support.
- Respond to customer complaints and resolve any technical problems to ensure that company products are working effectively and the customer is satisfied with the service provided.

- Provide feedback to any relevant company departments about complaints and problems to try to ensure that these do not arise in the future.
- Investigate any claims made against the company by the customer and negotiate an acceptable settlement where possible.
- Organize site visits and product trials for prospective customers and report results to relevant managers in the company.

## TRANSPORT AND DISTRIBUTION

- Maintain a close liaison with existing and potential customers to ensure that they are completely satisfied with the service provided.
- Maintain regular contact with customers to resolve any problems, identify new business opportunities and improve service levels and efficiency.

## VOLUNTARY SECTOR

- Respond to inquiries from donors and potential donors relating to donations.
- Give presentations on the work of the organization to encourage fundraising and to promote the aims and objectives of the organization.
- Raise and maintain awareness of the organization's activities to ensure maximum publicity and to encourage donations.
- Develop policies and processes which directly contribute to the promotion of the organization's public image.
- Develop and maintain effective contacts with a wide range of external bodies, including contractors and suppliers, to ensure wide publicity and cost-effective support for the organization's policies and activities.

# 19

# Management of finance and budgets

## ADMINISTRATION AND MANAGEMENT

- Develop and monitor budgets for all major organization development projects.
- Prepare, gain acceptance, and monitor the implementation of the annual budget to ensure that budget targets are met, that revenue flows are maximized and that fixed costs are minimized.
- Develop and control the annual budget for all central support services.
- Prepare the annual budget for office services and monitor expenditure against this budget.

## ENGINEERING AND PRODUCTION

- Develop the department's budget in discussion with other managers and maintain any necessary systems and processes to ensure effective budget monitoring and control.

- Develop and monitor the product development budget to ensure that all projects are effectively costed.
- Assist in the preparation and monitoring of budgets to ensure that maintenance is carried out within agreed costs.
- Monitor and control the factory budget to ensure that all financial and business objectives are met.
- Develop and control the budget for the department to ensure that the department has all the resources required to meet its objectives within agreed financial parameters.
- Prepare and monitor budgets to ensure that the optimum use is made of production resources.
- Control all departmental budgets and resources to ensure that these operate cost-effectively and in accordance with quality standards.
- Assist in the preparation of annual budgets.
- Monitor the maintenance budget to ensure that all costs are kept within the agreed limits.

## ESTATES AND SURVEYING

- Develop and monitor an annual operating budget to ensure that all financial targets are met, and regulations complied with, in relation to the function.
- Monitor the maintenance budget to ensure that this is appropriately allocated and so that the company achieves the best value for money.
- Maintain all necessary financial records relating to contracts to ensure that payments are made at the appropriate time.

## HUMAN RESOURCES/PERSONNEL

- Develop and monitor budgets for all major organization development projects.
- Develop and monitor the personnel budget to ensure that personnel services are provided at the appropriate level consistent with the attainment of the company's corporate objectives.

- Develop and monitor the company's training budget to ensure that the best quality of training and development is provided within the established budget.

## INFORMATION TECHNOLOGY

- Develop an annual business plan and operating budget for the department and monitor the implementation of these to ensure that financial targets are met.
- Monitor and control the software development budget.

## LEGAL

- Develop and monitor an annual budget for the department to ensure that all financial targets are met and appropriate financial controls are in place.

## LEISURE SERVICES

- Provide counter and cash collection services to members the public and maintain records of the centre's income and expenditure.
- Process all invoices, claim forms, timesheets, and bills etc.
- Monitor and control all budgets and cash to ensure that the centre meets all established financial targets.

## PUBLIC RELATIONS AND MEDIA

- Develop and monitor the department's budget to ensure to ensure that the necessary financial resources are made available and that expenditure is kept within the prescribed limits.
- Monitor the department's budget to ensure that services provided are within agreed financial limits.
- Develop and monitor budgets for sales representatives and for advertising and conferences to ensure that these deliver the results required.

# PURCHASING AND STORES

- Maintain the central purchasing budget to ensure the effective monitoring and control of all purchases.

# RESEARCH AND DEVELOPMENT (R&D) AND SCIENCE

- Develop and control the budget for the department to ensure that all financial and cost objectives are met and targets are achieved within overall cost constraints.
- Oversee the research budget ensuring that any research projects undertaken are relevant, accurately costed and provide value for money.

# SALES AND MARKETING

- Monitor and control the budget for the area to ensure that all financial targets are met and that all necessary financial controls are in place to comply with company and regulatory requirements.
- Direct and control the directorate's finances to ensure that all financial targets are met and to promote effective budgeting and cost control.
- Develop and implement the department's budget to ensure that all business objectives are attained.
- Oversee the department's finances to ensure that all revenue, profit and cost targets are met.
- Control and monitor the directorate's finances to ensure effective budgeting and cost control.
- Develop and control the company budget for marketing promotions.
- Monitor the product development budget to ensure that all targets are met within specified budget limits.
- Develop and control the budget for the sales function to ensure that all financial targets are met and that all necessary financial controls are in place to comply with company and regulatory requirements.

# TRANSPORT AND DISTRIBUTION

- Develop and maintain the transport budget to ensure that services are provided to the required standard and within budgeted limits.

# VOLUNTARY SECTOR

- Maintain budgetary and cost records relating to appeals and donations.
- Oversee all bank accounts relating to income received and closely monitor cash balances and transfers from and into accounts.
- Develop and control the department's budget to ensure that services are provided within agreed financial limits.
- Maintain all necessary budgetary and cost records to ensure that the costs of voluntary support are accurately recorded.

# 20

# Project management

## ADMINISTRATION AND MANAGEMENT

- Develop and control multidisciplinary teams to ensure that action plans are implemented and changes achieved that will support the organization's core objectives.

## ENGINEERING AND PRODUCTION

- Direct and control engineering projects to ensure that they are completed to the standards required within agreed timescales and to the agreed budget level.
- Assist in the coordination of projects to ensure that environmental issues are taken into account.
- Coordinate projects across the company to determine project objectives and timetable and to ensure that all objectives are met within agreed timescales and budgets.
- Maintain regular contact with operational managers and external contractors to define the scope of projects and the resulting implementation plans.

- Define, in consultation with operational managers, the benefits, costs, key result areas and success criteria for defined projects.
- Define project stages and the objectives and costs associated with each stage.
- Identify the resources required at each project stage to meet project objectives and negotiate the release of these resources with operational managers.
- Assess the impact of any one project on other concurrent projects and allocate resources as necessary to achieve the optimum results.
- Monitor and report on project progress in a structured manner, drawing particular attention to deviations from the original project plan.
- Maintain and update the project plan.
- Direct and control the project team to ensure that they achieve their objectives and that the best possible use is made of available staff resources.
- Review all projects and modify performance measures as necessary.

## ESTATES AND SURVEYING

- Coordinate major projects through a team to ensure that all target dates are met to the required standards and within agreed costs.
- Coordinate more complex projects to ensure that they are achieved within budgetary and time constraints and in accordance with regulations.
- Supervise the implementation of contracts for the maintenance and modernization of buildings to ensure that work is carried out to the required standards and within agreed budgets and time-scales.
- Measure and value completed projects and authorize payment provided the contract is within the agreed specifications.

## FINANCE AND ACCOUNTANCY

- Decide what data is required for any particular project and determine the most appropriate methods for the collection and analysis of this data.

- Carry out various ad hoc projects in relation to financial and performance data.

## HUMAN RESOURCES/PERSONNEL

- Develop and monitor budgets for all major organization development projects.

## INFORMATION TECHNOLOGY

- Plan and coordinate major IT projects within the organization to ensure that effective IT solutions are delivered within agreed timescales and costs.
- Assist in the development of IT project plans across the organization to ensure that effective systems are introduced to meet identified needs.
- Monitor the implementation of IT projects to ensure that all targets are reached and that the overall project is completed in accordance with agreed timescales and costs.
- Identify user requirements and develop project and product specifications that will ensure that these requirements are met.
- Develop and implement any necessary procedures and documentation required to support new IT systems and procedures.
- Conduct post-project evaluations to ensure that systems implemented are operating effectively and providing the services required by users.
- Represent the department on project teams to ensure that the best possible advice is given about the implications of any new IT systems and proposed changes.

## PUBLIC RELATIONS AND MEDIA

- Direct and monitor external projects to ensure that activities are carried out to the required standard, within agreed budgets, and that targets are met.

# RESEARCH AND DEVELOPMENT (R&D) AND SCIENCE

- Direct and control research projects to ensure that they deliver timely and cost-effective results which enhance the effectiveness of the company and its products.
- Oversee the research budget, ensuring that any research projects undertaken are relevant, accurately costed and provide value for money.

# TRANSPORT AND DISTRIBUTION

- Carry out projects relating to the use of the warehouse and logistics to improve operational effectiveness.

# 21

# Research and development

## ADMINISTRATION AND MANAGEMENT

- Develop and maintain research and development programmes to ensure that the company remains at the forefront in the industry, applies the most cost-effective methods and approaches, provides leading-edge products and services and retains its competitive edge.

## ENGINEERING AND PRODUCTION

- Introduce and oversee a process for the research and design of new products and modifications to existing products to ensure continuous improvement.
- Research customer requirements to ensure that products meet the purposes for which they are designed and satisfy those requirements.
- Undertake studies and trials of chemicals and instruments to improve production processes, unit costs, quality and safety.

- Undertake all necessary research to keep abreast of developments in the fields of total quality management and continuous improvement to ensure that the company maintains its competitive position.
- Research and compile information relating to company products and services to enable the preparation of accurate and up-to-date technical documentation.
- Collect technical and other information about competitors' products to ensure that the company maintains its competitive position.
- Carry out and commission research and advise on soil mechanics, hydraulics, water and waste water treatment processes and other related engineering matters to ensure that decisions are made on the basis of the best possible information.
- Design procedures to test existing products and equipment to identify areas for improvement.
- Maintain an awareness of new developments in technology and relevant production processes and evaluate and apply those that may be of benefit to the company.
- Maintain knowledge of new developments in maintenance practices and procedures to ensure that there is continuous improvement in maintenance standards.
- Maintain knowledge of new developments in production processes and propose modifications to plant and equipment so that the company makes the best use of technological developments in its sector.
- Maintain an awareness of production techniques and recommend any changes that might improve the quality or volume of output without compromising safety or environmental standards.
- Regularly review all working practices, procedures and equipment to ensure that they are the most efficient and effective available.
- Maintain an awareness of developments in the field of health and safety to ensure that the company continues to comply with best practice and legal requirements.
- Maintain an up-to-date knowledge of environmental standards, legislation and relevant technology to ensure that the company complies with best practice.

- Maintain an awareness of technical developments in the industry to ensure that the company maintains its competitive position.
- Collect technical and other information about competitors' products to ensure that the company maintains its competitive position.
- Maintain an awareness of developments in company products and those produced by competitors to ensure that the company continues to provide up-to-date products and services.
- Research and compile information relating to company products and services to be able to produce accurate and up-to-date technical documentation.
- Monitor feedback from customers and staff to ensure that technical documentation is clear and accurate.
- Research customer requirements to ensure that products meet the purposes for which they are designed and satisfy those requirements.

## ESTATES AND SURVEYING

- Maintain an awareness of developments in the field of architecture so that up-to-date and accurate advice can be given to clients.
- Maintain an awareness of developments in the field of surveying and property maintenance to ensure the provision of comprehensive and accurate advice in these areas.
- Maintain an awareness of developments in the field of quantity surveying and up-to-date knowledge of costs of construction materials to ensure that advice is reliable.

## FINANCE AND ACCOUNTANCY

- Analyse and interpret data using statistical, financial, economic and other appropriate techniques and advise managers on the appropriate actions and policies to be pursued in the light of these findings.
- Maintain an awareness of developments in the actuarial field to ensure that the latest techniques and approaches are applied.

- Carry out any necessary internal audit reviews and monitor the financial effectiveness of systems and controls.
- Keep up to date with any developments in financial management which might affect how the company's finances are managed or its statutory obligations.
- Maintain an awareness of developments in the field of management accountancy to ensure the continued provision of a high-quality professional service.
- Keep abreast of all developments relating to payroll law and administration to ensure that the company complies with its statutory obligations and follows best practice.

# FINANCIAL SERVICES

- Continually reassess the operational risk inherent in the business, taking account of changing economic or market conditions, legal and regulatory requirements, operating procedures and practices, and the impact of new technology.
- Analyse and monitor market trends to be able to make recommendations about investments.
- Research general developments in markets to try to forecast trends.
- Maintain an awareness of economic, financial and political developments which might affect market trends.
- Research the economic, financial, political and other factors affecting markets and make appropriate recommendations to maximize investment returns to the company.
- Maintain detailed and up-to-date knowledge of all current tax legislation and other matters which might impact on the company's tax liabilities.
- Analyse risks by obtaining information from clients and other sources to determine appropriate premium levels.
- Maintain a sound knowledge of competitors by thoroughly analysing market position, products and rates etc.
- Undertake any necessary checks and research on prospective clients to provide the information required for accurate risk assessment.

- Undertake any necessary research and provide expertise and advice on any matters of general concern and interest to the company in the underwriting and claims fields.

# HUMAN RESOURCES/PERSONNEL

- Carry out and participate in salary surveys, and analyse data, to ensure that the organization has accurate and up-to-date information relating to external pay relativities.
- Carry out or commission research on reward issues to ensure that the organization is applying policies that are in line with market practice.
- Keep up to date with developments in the field of reward to ensure that the organization continues to apply the best reward practices.
- Maintain an awareness of developments in the fields of organization change and development to ensure that the organization continues to take advantage of the latest thinking in these areas.
- Commission research in the field of organization development and change to ensure that the organization implements policies and approaches that will improve operational effectiveness.
- Carry out research to provide information to support negotiations on pay and conditions.
- Maintain up-to-date knowledge about employment law as it relates to employee relations.
- Maintain an awareness of developments in the field of health and safety to ensure that the company continues to comply with best practice and legal requirements.
- Keep up to date with developments in the fields of job evaluation, equal value and related employment law to ensure that the organization continues to have accurate advice.
- Maintain an awareness of the requirements of employment legislation to ensure that the company complies with all legal requirements and to provide sound advice to management.
- Research and develop personnel policies which will ensure that the company recruits and retains a pool of well-trained and highly motivated staff.

- Undertake any necessary market research to ensure that the service provided is up to date and appropriate to clients' needs.
- Keep up to date with the latest developments in the field of recruitment and selection.
- Maintain an awareness of developments in the training and development field to ensure that the company continues to take advantage of best practice.

# INFORMATION TECHNOLOGY

- Maintain an awareness of developments in the computing field to ensure that the company continues to apply the technology most appropriate to its needs.
- Maintain an awareness of developments in the storage and handling of data and review the application of new technologies to improve administrative processes.
- Keep up to date with developments in programming to ensure that the company continues to take advantage of new ideas and developments.
- Develop a research and development programme to review all new and potential software applications.
- Maintain an awareness of developments in relation to software so that the company maintains its competitive position.

# LEGAL

- Carry out research and prepare reports on any legal issues to support the more senior members of the team.
- Maintain an awareness of developments in the legal field relevant to the organization, including reviewing and reporting on the implications of any new legislation.
- Carry out research and prepare reports on any legally complex issues to ensure that the organization has full information about the legal implications of any decisions.

# PUBLIC RELATIONS AND MEDIA

- Research the marketability and sales potential of proposals and/ or scripts and prepare a report to the publishing committee.
- Research and draft articles for publication.
- Monitor media articles to ensure that the organization is kept aware of issues of significance.
- Research and implement technical developments in the production process and consult company staff on proposed changes to improve the overall efficiency and effectiveness of the process.
- Maintain an awareness of developments in the field of public relations.
- Keep abreast of developments within the field of public relations to ensure that the organization maintains the highest standards of public relations.
- Research and develop news items and stories to about the organization's activities and services to promote a positive image of the organization and to raise its profile.
- Research and prepare briefing notes to ensure that managers have all relevant information when addressing press and media enquiries.
- Maintain up-to-date knowledge of developments in the book trade and keep colleagues informed of these so that the company maintains its competitive position.

# PURCHASING AND STORES

- Maintain an awareness of any developments in the field of central purchasing or with suppliers to ensure that the company continues to apply the most effective policies and procedures.

# SALES AND MARKETING

- Research new sales opportunities within the existing portfolio of accounts and identify new potential customers within the allocated sales area.

- Maintain an awareness of developments in sales generation and product development.
- Maintain an awareness of developments in sales techniques and technology to ensure that the company maintains and develops its competitive position.
- Monitor the sales performance of competitors to ensure that the company maintains and develops its competitive position.
- Carry out or commission surveys of customer satisfaction to identify the scope for improvements in product quality and service delivery.
- Carry out or commission research in the company's existing and potential markets to identify new opportunities.
- Maintain an awareness of developments in the fields of product marketing and research to ensure that the company continues to compete effectively.
- Oversee research into new and established markets to develop products and services that meet market demands and which are consistent with the company's corporate strategy.
- Maintain an awareness of developments in the field of credit management so that the company maintains up-to-date policies and continues to comply with relevant regulations.
- Recommend to sales and marketing and research and development staff any identified market needs for new or enhanced products.
- Research and identify new business opportunities to ensure sustained growth.
- Analyse trends in the business environment, help to develop products that are responsive to market demands, and identify new market opportunities.
- Develop and implement a market research policy that will enable the company to identify sales opportunities.
- Carry out research, analyse results and produce reports identifying relevant market trends and recommending appropriate policies and actions to be implemented by the company.
- Monitor research results to ensure that the policies and procedures adopted meet the company's requirements.
- Support the production, sales and marketing functions, by providing them with research results that will assist in decision making.

- Provide a source of expertise to managers and staff on carrying out market research.
- Maintain an awareness of developments in the field of market research to ensure that the company continues to apply the most effective policies and approaches.
- Monitor competitor activity in relation to national accounts and ensure that the appropriate responses are developed to any perceived threats to business.
- Maintain an awareness of developments in products and in the industry in general and pass any relevant findings to the appropriate departments.

## TRANSPORT AND DISTRIBUTION

- Maintain up-to-date knowledge of changes in legislation relating to cars and of the latest developments from manufacturers.

## VOLUNTARY SECTOR

- Research public and private sector organizations to maximize grant income and to identify potential donors.
- Keep abreast of developments within the field of public relations to ensure that the organization maintains the highest standards of public relations.

# 22

# Strategy development

## ADMINISTRATION AND MANAGEMENT

- Lead in the development of strategies, policies and processes across all functions that will help to achieve the company's mission and core objectives.
- Prepare a corporate plan and annual business plan and monitor progress against these plans to ensure that the company attains its objectives as cost-effectively and efficiently as possible.
- Develop and maintain an effective marketing and public relations strategy to promote the products, services and image of the company in the wider community.
- Contribute to the development of association policies which reflect the needs and objectives of association members.

## ENGINEERING AND PRODUCTION

- Develop the company's strategy in relation to engineering and ensure that all maintenance standards are adhered to by staff and contractors.

- Assist in the development of a strategy to ensure that the company complies with the best environmental standards and relevant legislation.
- Develop and implement short- and long-term plans to ensure that the factory has the necessary resources to meet business objectives.
- Contribute to the development of the company's corporate strategy and lead strategy development in the areas of production, purchasing and distribution to ensure that company achieves its short- and long-term objectives.
- Develop strategies and processes to ensure that total quality is promoted throughout the company.
- Develop policies and procedures to ensure the health and safety of all employees, contractors, and visitors to the company.

## ESTATES AND SURVEYING

- Contribute to the development of the company's strategic plan, particularly in relation to the effective use of the company's properties.

## FINANCE AND ACCOUNTANCY

- Contribute to the achievement of the company's business objectives by providing advice and guidance on financial strategy.
- Assist in the development of business plans to enable the company to meet its corporate objectives.
- Contribute to the development of the company's corporate strategy and develop and implement the financial and IS strategies to ensure the attainment and delivery of plans and objectives.

## FINANCIAL SERVICES

- Oversee the analysis and monitoring of market trends to be able to make recommendations about investment policy.

- Develop and implement all necessary policies and procedures to ensure the effective and optimal planning and management of the company's tax liabilities.
- Contribute to the company's underwriting policy to ensure that mortality and morbidity results are satisfactory.

# HUMAN RESOURCES/PERSONNEL

- Develop and implement reward policies and procedures which ensure that the organization is able to attract and retain the required number of staff with the appropriate skills and experience to be able to achieve its business objectives.
- Contribute to the development of strategies that will help to achieve the organization's mission and core objectives.
- Develop and implement all necessary policies and procedures to promote effective communication between management and staff and to encourage harmonious industrial relations.
- Develop policies and procedures to ensure the health and safety of all employees, contractors, and visitors to the company.
- Develop and implement policies and procedures to ensure that the organization's staffing needs are met.
- Contribute to the development of the company's corporate strategy, particularly by advising on the human resource implications of strategic decisions.
- Develop and maintain appropriate and effective personnel strategies and ensure that these are communicated and implemented throughout the company in a way that supports corporate objectives.
- Develop and maintain a remuneration strategy and appropriate terms and conditions of employment to ensure that the company is able to attract, retain and motivate staff.
- Develop and maintain all necessary training policies and procedures to ensure that all staff are trained and developed to the standards required.
- Develop and implement personnel policies to support business goals and to ensure that the company complies with legal requirements and best practice.

- Research and develop personnel policies which will ensure that the company recruits and retains a pool of well-trained and highly motivated staff.
- Identify the company's staffing needs and develop policies and procedures to ensure that the required numbers and types of staff are recruited within agreed budgets to meet operational requirements.
- Recommend and implement reward policies and structures which ensure the effective recruitment and retention of high quality employees.
- Assist in the development of personnel policies and procedures to ensure that the company follows best practice and avoids infringing employment law.
- Develop a training and development strategy for the company to support the company's business plan and to ensure that staff have the necessary skills to meet their objectives and have the opportunity to develop to the maximum of their potential.

# INFORMATION TECHNOLOGY

- Contribute to the development of the company's strategic and business plans, particularly in relation to information technology and communications systems, in support of the company's mission and core objectives.
- Develop and implement an information technology strategy to support the financial and business objectives of the company.

# PUBLIC RELATIONS AND MEDIA

- Give strategic advice to the managers and staff in relation to their dealings with the media, to promote the public profile of the organization.
- Develop policies and processes which directly contribute to the promotion of the organization's public image.
- Develop and implement the company's publishing strategy to ensure the achievement of the company's corporate objectives and to maximize revenues from the sale of publications.

# PURCHASING AND STORES

- Assist in the development of a central purchasing policy to ensure that the company makes the best use of its purchasing power.
- Develop and implement all necessary policies and procedures to ensure that the purchasing function operates effectively.

# RESEARCH AND DEVELOPMENT (R&D) AND SCIENCE

- Contribute to the development of the company's corporate strategy.
- Contribute to the development of a research and development strategy for the organization.
- Assist in the development of the organization's research policies to ensure that these support the overall mission and objectives.
- Assist in the development of the organization's economic policies to ensure that these support the overall mission and objectives.

# SALES AND MARKETING

- Develop and implement all necessary commercial policies and procedures to ensure the effective promotion and marketing of the company and to meet business objectives.
- Contribute to the development of the company's corporate strategy, as part of the corporate management team, with particular reference to the development of the company's commercial objectives.
- Develop and implement a customer service strategy which provides total customer satisfaction and meets corporate objectives.
- Develop all necessary policies and procedures to ensure the effective promotion and marketing of the company.
- Assist in formulating and monitoring the annual business plan to ensure the long- term success and viability of the company and the attainment of corporate objectives.
- Advise the company, as part of the corporate management team, on the development of new initiatives and the promotion and

marketing of products to ensure the achievement of the company's business plan and corporate objectives.

- Contribute to the development of the company's corporate strategy, particularly in relation to sales objectives.
- Develop and implement sales strategies that enable the company to achieve its corporate objectives.

## TRANSPORT AND DISTRIBUTION

- Assist in the development of the company's transport strategy to ensure the provision of the best possible quality of service and to maximize company profitability.

## VOLUNTARY SECTOR

- Develop and implement a national strategy to maximize the fund income to the organization.

# 23

# Supervision and management

## ADMINISTRATION AND MANAGEMENT

- Recruit and motivate business-orientated teams accountable for the achievement of corporate and individual targets, ensuring that comprehensive performance appraisal and development opportunities are provided in accordance with the company's human resources strategy and employment policies.
- Supervise all clerical, typing, secretarial and support staff to ensure that they are appropriately trained and carry out their responsibilities to the required standards.
- Oversee the opening and distribution of internal and external post.
- Supervise reception and switchboard staff to ensure that there is appropriate cover at all times.
- Supervise the provision of word processing and typing services to all staff.
- Oversee the provision of a comprehensive and reliable filing and photocopying service.

- Direct and control the work and resources of the company and ensure the recruitment and retention of the required numbers and types of well-motivated, trained and developed staff to ensure that it achieves its mission and objectives.
- Oversee the arrangements for the conduct of elections to the Board and committees.
- Direct and control the staff of the department to ensure that they are appropriately motivated and trained and that they carry out their responsibilities to the required standards.
- Develop and implement all necessary administrative policies and procedures to ensure that the company continues to operate efficiently and effectively.
- Direct and control all central services to ensure that they provide managers and staff with the level of support they require.
- Monitor the performance of all central services to ensure that they operate to a high standard and to identify any areas of potential improvement.
- Supervise and train the staff of the ............. to ensure that they carry out their responsibilities to the required standards.
- Supervise the office cleaning work carried out by in-house staff or by contractors to ensure that it is carried out to the required standards.
- Monitor the performance of contractors to ensure that work is carried out to the required standards.
- Negotiate and agree cleaning services for the building and monitor the work carried out to ensure that it is of the required standards.
- Supervise the work of administrative support staff to ensure that they provide the administrative services required by the company to the required standards.
- Supervise the distribution of incoming mail and the efficient despatch of outgoing mail.

## ENGINEERING AND PRODUCTION

- Direct and control the staff of the engineering function to ensure that all processes, plant, equipment and buildings are maintained to agreed standards.

- Monitor maintenance work to ensure that it is carried out to the required standards and within agreed budget levels.
- Direct and control engineering projects to ensure that they are completed to the standards required within agreed timescales and to the agreed budget level.
- Recruit, train and motivate maintenance staff to ensure that they carry out their responsibilities to the required standards.
- Investigate and resolve any disciplinary or employee relations issues to ensure that all processes, plant and equipment continue to be maintained to the standards necessary to meet operational requirements.
- Plan the installation of products and services to ensure that these are completed to the required standards and within the agreed timescale.
- Inspect completed installations to ensure that these have been undertaken to the required standards.
- Maintain regular contact with installers and subcontractors to ensure that they are appropriately trained and carry out contract work to the required standards.
- Oversee the design of products and test these to ensure that they meet all quality standards and specifications and satisfy customer requirements.
- Oversee the production of comprehensive documentation and information about products to ensure that customers are given all the required information for effective product use.
- Continuously review product performance and feedback from customers to develop any necessary improvements to products.
- Introduce and oversee a process for the research and design of new products and modifications to existing products to ensure continuous improvement.
- Train company staff in the operation and maintenance of products and equipment.
- Supervise external contractors and internal workers as required.
- Ensure that all work is carried out in accordance with company safety rules and health and safety legislation.
- Ensure that all work is carried out in accordance with relevant environmental standards.

- Assist in the coordination of projects to ensure that environmental issues are taken into account.
- Direct and control all factory staff to ensure that they are properly motivated, trained and developed, and carry out their responsibilities to the required standards and in accordance with health, safety and hygiene standards.
- Organize all production operations to ensure that output and quality targets are achieved and that all relevant health, safety and hygiene standards are observed.
- Oversee all site cleaning to ensure that this is in accordance with the specified standards.
- Plan, organize and control all maintenance work within the company to ensure that plant and equipment is maintained to the required standards of quality and availability.
- Supervise and train all maintenance staff to ensure that they carry out their duties effectively and to maintain effective working relationships.
- Monitor all maintenance work to ensure that it complies with all health and safety requirements.
- Direct and control all manufacturing staff to ensure that they are appropriately motivated and trained and carry out their responsibilities to the required standards.
- Oversee all manufacturing operations to ensure that they meet agreed production plans, product quality and cost standards.
- Direct and control all production, purchasing and distribution employees to ensure that they are appropriately motivated and trained and carry their responsibilities to the required standards.
- Direct and control the production function to ensure that finished goods of the required standards are available to customers within agreed costs and at the right times.
- Direct and control the purchasing function to ensure that the company has all the resources required for production purposes within agreed costs and quality standards and at the right times.
- Direct and control the warehousing and distribution functions to ensure that customers are supplied with the right quantities of goods at the right times.
- Supervise process personnel to ensure that they receive any necessary training and to resolve any production problems.

- Direct and control the staff of the department to ensure that they are appropriately trained and motivated and carry out their responsibilities to the required standards.
- Oversee all operating processes to ensure that the most efficient and effective use is made of plant and equipment and that safety standards are adhered to.
- Supervise a team of operatives to ensure that they carry out their work effectively and safely.
- Monitor the volume and quality of output to ensure that these are to the standards required.
- Monitor manning levels on production equipment and make changes as necessary in the event of staff absence.
- Train operators in the production process to ensure that they work efficiently and safely.
- Monitor the working environment to ensure that company safety policies and health and safety regulations are complied with and to provide a safe and healthy working environment.
- Direct and control the project team to ensure that they achieve their objectives and that the best possible use is made of available staff resources.
- Direct and control the staff of the quality department to ensure that they are well motivated and receive all necessary training and development to enable them to carry out their responsibilities to the required standards.
- Supervise shift personnel to ensure that they carry out their responsibilities to the required standards and within safety rules and regulations.
- Monitor output to ensure that targets have been achieved in terms of the required quality and volume.
- Coordinate maintenance activities to ensure that there is a minimum of downtime and lost production.
- Identify and resolve technical and personnel problems to ensure that continuous production is maintained.
- Provide any necessary training and advice to shift personnel to ensure that they carry out their responsibilities effectively.

# ESTATES AND SURVEYING

- Negotiate and oversee contracts with builders to ensure that work is carried out to the appropriate standards and in accordance with agreed timescales and costs.
- Monitor and audit work carried out by contractors to ensure that it is of the required standards.
- Coordinate major projects through a team to ensure that all target dates are met to the required standards and within agreed costs.
- Direct and control the staff of the department to ensure that they are appropriately trained and motivated and carry out their responsibilities to the required standards.
- Coordinate more complex projects to ensure that they are achieved within budgetary and time constraints and in accordance with regulations.
- Oversee the preparation of tender documentation, including the compilation of schedules of rates, schedules of works, designs, drawings, conditions of contracts, specifications etc and make recommendations on tenders received.
- Supervise the implementation of contracts for the maintenance and modernization of buildings to ensure that work is carried out to the required standards and within agreed budgets and time-scales.
- Oversee the maintenance of the company's properties to ensure that they are of the required standard.
- Commission any necessary work required to maintain properties to the standards required, conforming to agreed procedures, and monitor any such work to ensure that it is carried out to the required standards and within the agreed budget.
- Supervise the team to ensure that they are appropriately trained and motivated and carry out their responsibilities to the required standards.

# FINANCE AND ACCOUNTANCY

- Direct and control the .............. team to ensure that they are appropriately motivated and trained and carry out their responsibilities to the required standards.

413

- Oversee the preparation of the company's financial accounts to ensure that these are presented accurately and on time.
- Supervise accountancy staff to ensure that they are appropriately motivated and trained and carry out their responsibilities effectively.
- Supervise the accurate and timely payment of all staff salaries and expenses, making the appropriate statutory deductions.
- Supervise the administration of the permanent health insurance scheme and the pension scheme.
- Supervise the administration of the Statutory Sick Pay scheme, Statutory Maternity Pay and Statutory Paternity Pay schemes.
- Oversee the timely and accurate submission of all statutory returns to the Inland Revenue and other government departments.
- Supervise payroll staff to ensure that they are appropriately motivated and trained and carry out their responsibilities effectively.
- Oversee the preparation of statistical returns and financial analysis on a range of topics for internal and external use.
- Oversee the administration of any loans and repayments, including maintaining liaison with brokers and lenders.
- Supervise audit staff to ensure that they carry out their responsibilities effectively.
- Supervise the staff of the section to ensure that all required training and development is received and that work is carried out to the required standards.
- Oversee the day-to-day operations of the purchase ledger.
- Supervise the petty cash system.

## FINANCIAL SERVICES

- Direct and control the branch team to ensure that they are appropriately motivated and trained and that they achieve their objectives.
- Direct and control a team of analysts to ensure that they are appropriately motivated and trained and carry out their responsibilities the required standards.

- Oversee the analysis and monitoring of market trends to be able to make recommendations about investment policy.
- Oversee the compilation and despatch of all relevant statutory returns, ensuring that these are accurate and meet all deadlines.
- Direct and control the underwriting and claims staff to ensure that they are appropriately motivated and receive all the training and development necessary to carry out their roles effectively.

## HUMAN RESOURCES/PERSONNEL

- Direct and control the staff of the department to ensure that they are appropriately motivated and trained and carry out their responsibilities to the required standards.
- Supervise employee relations staff to ensure that they are appropriately motivated and trained and carry out their responsibilities to the required standards.
- Direct and control the staff of the personnel department to ensure that they undertake their responsibilities effectively and within budget.
- Supervise the process for the placing of advertisements for all internal and external vacancies.
- Oversee all administrative arrangements relating to the recruitment and selection process, including arranging tests and providing suitable arrangements for applicants with special needs.
- Oversee the development of effective processes for the evaluation of all training and development provided.
- Oversee the maintenance of all necessary training and development records.

## INFORMATION TECHNOLOGY

- Supervise data entry staff to ensure that they are appropriately trained and carry out their tasks to the required standards.
- Organize and control the central database and all data input and output to ensure that information required for management decision making and statutory compliance is accurate and provided at the right time.

- Direct and control the staff of the information technology and communications department to ensure that they are well motivated and receive all necessary training and development to enable them to carry out their responsibilities to the required standards.
- Oversee the management of all data and information flows within the company to ensure that comprehensive and accurate management information is available as required.
- Manage systems projects to ensure that results are delivered within agreed timescales and budgets.

# LEGAL

- Assist in organizing and controlling the work of the department to ensure that staff are appropriately trained and motivated and carry out their responsibilities to the required standards.
- Supervise legal staff to ensure that they carry out their responsibilities to the required standards and receive all necessary training and development.

# LEISURE SERVICES

- Supervise the staff of the centre to ensure that they receive all necessary training and instruction and carry out their responsibilities to the required standards.
- Supervise cleaners and other contractors to ensure that work is carried out to the required standards.

# PUBLIC RELATIONS AND MEDIA

- Oversee all stages of the production of manuscripts and reprints, maintaining a constant liaison with the author, commissioning editor and production department as necessary.
- Monitor all stages of the production process to ensure that the production schedule is adhered to.

- Control the process for the production of publications, maintaining regular contact with external designers and printers, to ensure that publications are produced to the required standards and within agreed deadlines.
- Control the production and distribution of promotional material within agreed budget limits.
- Control the process for the production of publications to ensure that they are produced to the required standards and at the right time.
- Oversee all stages of the production process to ensure that publications are produced on time to the required standards and within budget.
- Direct and control the staff of the Public Relations Department to ensure that they achieve their objectives and receive all appropriate training and development.
- Direct and monitor external projects to ensure that activities are carried out to the required standards, within agreed budgets, and that targets are met.
- Oversee the development and maintenance of the photograph library, Web site, publications and other communications/marketing tools.
- Supervise public relations staff to ensure that they are appropriately motivated and trained and carry out their responsibilities to the required standards.
- Develop and direct campaigns for the promotion of the organization's policies.
- Direct and control the staff of the publishing function to ensure that they achieve their objectives and receive all appropriate training and development.
- Direct and control the production process to ensure that publications are produced on time to the required standards and within budget.
- Direct and monitor external projects to ensure that activities are carried out to the required standards, within agreed budgets, and that targets are met.
- Oversee the organization of sales conferences, sales meetings and other sales promotions to ensure that company products are effectively promoted.

- Oversee key accounts to keep them informed of publications and to maximize sales.

## PURCHASING AND STORES

- Direct and control purchasing staff to ensure that they are well motivated and trained and that they carry out their responsibilities to the required standards.

## RESEARCH AND DEVELOPMENT (R&D) AND SCIENCE

- Direct, organize and train the pharmacists working in the dispensary to ensure that the dispensary operates effectively and that all staff perform their duties to the required standards.
- Monitor the workload in the dispensary, taking any necessary action to ensure that all outputs are achieved to the required standards.
- Direct and control staff to ensure that they are appropriately motivated and trained and carry out their responsibilities to the required standards.
- Direct and control the staff of the R&D Department to ensure that they carry out their responsibilities effectively and that there is a safe and healthy work environment.
- Direct and control research projects to ensure that they deliver timely and cost-effective results which enhance the effectiveness of the company and its products.
- Supervise a team of research and support staff ensuring that they are appropriately trained and motivated and carry out their responsibilities to the required standards.
- Oversee the research budget, ensuring that any research projects undertaken are relevant, accurately costed and provide value for money.
- Supervise a team of economists and support staff, ensuring that they are appropriately trained and motivated and carry out their responsibilities to the required standards.

# SALES AND MARKETING

- Organize and control area sales staff to ensure that they are appropriately motivated and trained to meet all sales targets and that they carry out their responsibilities to the required standards.
- Supervise call centre staff to ensure that they are appropriately motivated and trained and carry out their responsibilities to the required standards.
- Allocate workload to call centre staff, ensuring that it is evenly distributed and that business targets are met.
- Oversee research into new and established markets to develop products and services that meet market demands and which are consistent with the company's corporate strategy.
- Direct and control the directorate's finances to ensure that all financial targets are met and to promote effective budgeting and cost control.
- Direct and control the staff of the directorate to ensure that they are appropriately motivated and trained and are working towards the achievement of the company's corporate objectives.
- Oversee the provision of help desk support to customers experiencing difficulties with company products.
- Direct and control the staff of the department to ensure that they are appropriately motivated and trained and carry out their responsibilities to the required standards.
- Oversee the department's finances to ensure that all revenue, profit and cost targets are met.
- Direct and control the staff of the directorate to ensure that they are appropriately motivated and trained and are working towards the achievement of the company's corporate objectives.
- Develop plans for the advertising and marketing of company products to raise the company's market profile and increase sales.
- Oversee the organization of promotional activities, ensuring that they are carried out efficiently and within agreed budgets, to raise the profile of the company and increase sales.
- Coordinate all marketing plans and activities with other managers and staff in the company to ensure that the plans are delivered effectively.

- Direct and control the staff of the product marketing department to ensure that they are appropriately motivated and trained and carry out their responsibilities to the required standards.
- Oversee research into new product developments to ensure that any required changes are made within the agreed timescale and budget.
- Direct and control the company's sales staff to ensure that they are appropriately motivated and trained to meet all sales targets and that they carry out their responsibilities to the required standards.
- Organize site visits and product trials for prospective customers and report results to relevant managers in the company.

## SECRETARIAL AND CLERICAL

- Supervise the company's secretarial staff to ensure that they are appropriately trained and carry out their responsibilities to the required standards.
- Oversee the operation of the company's telephone service, ensuring that all calls are dealt with promptly, courteously and efficiently.
- Organize a staffing rota to ensure that adequate cover is provided for the telephone service.
- Oversee the maintenance and the distribution of the internal telephone directory to ensure that users have up-to-date and accurate information.
- Oversee the work of a group of word processor operators to ensure that they produce typed material to a consistently high standard.
- Provide any necessary training and advice to staff to ensure that work is produced to the required standards.
- Assist in the selection of new staff, including organizing the appropriate aptitude tests.
- Oversee the maintenance of all machinery and equipment used and arrange emergency backup in the event of system failures, to ensure continuity of typing services.
- Maintain all holiday and sickness records for staff of the section.

# TRANSPORT AND DISTRIBUTION

- Oversee the administration of the company's car policy to ensure that it is complied with in all respects.
- Direct and control all depot operations to ensure that profitability targets are achieved and that full utilization is made of both vehicles and staff while maintaining the highest standards of safety and efficiency.
- Direct and control the staff of the depot to ensure that harmonious working relationships are maintained and to ensure that they are appropriately trained and motivated to carry out their responsibilities to the highest standards.
- Supervise garage and engineering staff to ensure that they are appropriately motivated and trained and carry out their responsibilities to the required standards.
- Oversee the management of contracts and provide advice on these to the company to ensure that effective relationships are maintained with suppliers and that contractual commitments are met.
- Oversee the provision of a comprehensive vehicle maintenance service to the company's vehicle fleet.
- Supervise staff in the garage to ensure that they are appropriately trained and motivated and carry out their responsibilities to the required standards.
- Oversee all vehicle maintenance operations to ensure that company vehicles are effectively maintained and serviced.
- Supervise a team of operatives to ensure that they carry out their work effectively and safely.
- Monitor the volume and quality of output to ensure that these are to the standards required.
- Monitor manning levels or make changes as necessary in the event of staff absence.
- Train operators in the packing process to ensure that they work efficiently and safely.
- Monitor the working environment to ensure that company and statutory hygiene and safety policies and regulations are complied with and to provide a safe and healthy working environment.
- Supervise staff to ensure that they carry out their responsibilities to the required standards and receive all required training.

- Oversee all goods in and ensure that these are unloaded and stored efficiently and safely.
- Oversee the despatch operation to ensure that it operates efficiently, effectively and safely and meets customer requirements.
- Oversee the use of the warehouse to ensure the maximum use of available space and a safe, efficient and profitable operation which meets customer and business needs.
- Oversee the use and maintenance of the company's vehicle fleet.
- Direct and control staff in transport depots to ensure that they carry out their responsibilities effectively and provide a high quality service to customers.
- Direct and control the use of the warehouse to ensure the maximum use of available space and a safe, efficient and profitable operation which meets customer and business needs.
- Direct and control the staff of the warehouse to ensure that they are appropriately trained and motivated and carry out their responsibilities to the required standards.

## VOLUNTARY SECTOR

- Direct and control fundraising staff to ensure that they are appropriately motivated and trained and carry out their responsibilities to the required standards.
- Direct and control public relations staff to ensure that they are appropriately motivated and trained and carry out their responsibilities to the required standards.
- Recruit and train volunteers to ensure that they are able to carry out the work required to the required standards.
- Provide support, advice and guidance to volunteers to ensure that they carry out their responsibilities effectively.

# Index of jobs by category

## ADMINISTRATION AND MANAGEMENT

1. Awards/grants officer
2. Business development director
3. Central services supervisor
4. Chauffeur
5. Chief executive
6. Committee administrator
7. Company secretary
8. Courier
9. Director of central services
10. Management consultant
11. Managing director
12. Member services manager
13. Nursery assistant
14. Nursery manager
15. Office maintenance worker
16. Office manager
17. VDU operator

# ENGINEERING AND PRODUCTION

1. Chief electrical engineer
2. Chief mechanical engineer
3. Civil engineer
4. Contract manager
5. Design manager
6. Development engineer
7. Draughtsperson
8. Electrical engineer
9. Electrical technician
10. Environmental manager
11. Factory manager
12. Hygiene officer
13. Maintenance supervisor
14. Manufacturing manager
15. Mechanical maintenance engineer
16. Operations director
17. Process auditor
18. Process chemist
19. Process engineer
20. Product technician
21. Production engineer
22. Production manager
23. Production operative
24. Production planner
25. Production supervisor
26. Project coordinator
27. Quality checker
28. Quality controller
29. Quality manager
30. Quality systems analyst
31. Repair technician
32. Safety manager
33. Service technician
34. Shift coordinator
35. Technical author
36. Technical manager

37.  Technical services manager
38.  Technical support engineer
39.  Water engineer

# ESTATES AND SURVEYING

1.  Architect
2.  Caretaker
3.  Carpenter
4.  Chief architect
5.  Chief surveyor
6.  Clerk of works
7.  Director of estates and surveying
8.  Electrician
9.  Gardener
10.  Maintenance manager
11.  Maintenance supervisor
12.  Maintenance worker
13.  Painter/decorator
14.  Plasterer
15.  Plumber
16.  Principal architect
17.  Principal surveyor
18.  Quantity surveyor
19.  Senior surveyor
20.  Surveyor

# FINANCE AND ACCOUNTANCY

1.  Accounts clerk
2.  Accounts clerk – controls and reconciliations
3.  Accounts supervisor
4.  Actuary
5.  Auditor
6.  Cashier
7.  Chief internal auditor
8.  Credit controller

9. Credit manager
10. Director of finance and information systems
11. Finance director
12. Financial accountant
13. Financial controller
14. Management accountant
15. Payroll assistant
16. Payroll supervisor
17. Principal accountant/section head
18. Sales ledger clerk
19. Senior accountant
20. Senior internal auditor
21. Systems accountant

## FINANCIAL SERVICES

1. Branch manager (bank)
2. Claims clerk
3. Investment analyst
4. Investment manager
5. Tax manager
6. Underwriter
7. Underwriting and claims manager
8. Underwriting clerk
9. Underwriting manager

## HUMAN RESOURCES/PERSONNEL

1. Compensation analyst
2. Compensation and benefits manager
3. Director of organization development
4. Employee relations manager
5. Employee relations officer
6. Health and safety manager
7. Human resource planning manager
8. Job analyst
9. Job evaluator

# LEISURE SERVICES

1. Administrative assistant
2. Leisure centre manager
3. Pool attendant
4. Recreation assistant

# PUBLIC RELATIONS AND MEDIA

1. Commissioning editor
2. Communications executive
3. Desk editor
4. Editor
5. Marketing executive
6. Media coordinator
7. Press officer
8. Production manager
9. Public relations director
10. Public relations manager
11. Public relations officer
12. Publicity executive
13. Publishing director
14. Sales manager

# PURCHASING AND STORES

1. Buyer
2. Materials controller
3. Purchasing manager
4. Stores manager

# RESEARCH AND DEVELOPMENT (R&D) AND SCIENCE

1. Analytical chemist
2. Archaeologist

3. Biologist
4. R&D director
5. Business development manager
6. Chief pharmacist
7. Economist
8. Geologist
9. Laboratory technician
10. Pharmacist
11. Product development manager
12. Microbiologist
13. Research manager
14. Researcher
15. Senior economist
16. Statistician

# SALES AND MARKETING

1. Area sales manager
2. Account manager
3. Brand manager
4. Business development manager
5. Call centre supervisor
6. Commercial director
7. Credit manager
8. Customer relations manager
9. Customer services director
10. Director of marketing
11. Estimator
12. Market researcher
13. Marketing communications manager
14. National accounts manager
15. Product marketing manager
16. Sales administrator
17. Sales director
18. Sales executive
19. Technical sales manager

# SECRETARIAL AND CLERICAL

1. Clerk/typist
2. Copy typist
3. Data input clerk/VDU operator
4. Filing clerk
5. Personal assistant/secretary to chief executive
6. Postal clerk
7. Receptionist
8. Receptionist and switchboard operator
9. Reprographics operator
10. Secretary
11. Telephone supervisor
12. Telephonist
13. Typing/word processing supervisor
14. Word processor operator

# TRANSPORT AND DISTRIBUTION

1. Car fleet manager
2. Depot manager
3. Fleet engineer
4. Garage manager
5. Packing supervisor
6. Supply chain manager
7. Transport manager
8. Warehouse manager
9. Warehouseman

# VOLUNTARY SECTOR

1. Company secretary (charity)
2. Donations administrator
3. Fundraiser
4. Fundraising assistant
5. Fundraising manager

6. Income clerk
7. Publications administrator
8. Publicity manager
9. Volunteer coordinator

# Index